Pure and Simple Origami

Marc Kirschenbaum

Fit to Print Publishing, Inc.
New York, NY

Pure and Simple Origami
Copyright © 2020
Fit To Print Publishing, Inc.

All rights reserved. No part of this publication may be reproduced, stored in a retrieval system or transmitted in any form or by any means, electronic, mechanical, photocopying, recording or otherwise, without the permission of the copyright holder.

ISBN 978-1-951146-15-3 (Paperback Edition)
ISBN 978-1-951146-16-0 (Hardcover Edition)

The diagrams in this book were produced with Macromedia's Freehand, and image processing was done with Adobe Photoshop. The Backtalk family of typefaces was used for the body text and the cover and headers use Helvetica. Ellen Cohen assisted with the cover design and provided valuable artistic assistance. Special thanks to Sara Adams for providing some of the papers used.

Contents

Introduction	5
Paper & Materials	6
Symbols & Terminology	8
Angel	14
Bumblebee	18
Butterfly	21
Calla Lily	24
Car	27
Dachshund	34
Dragon	37
Elephant	42
Fish	45
Frog	47
Guitar	50
Heart	55
Horse	57
Ladybug	60
Owl	67
Pencil	70
Plane	75
Ram	80
Sailboat	83
Santa Claus	85
Shirt	91
Skunk	97
Smiley Face	101
Sunflower	106
Teddy Bear	109
Tree	120
T-rex	123

Introduction

In the 1970's British origami historian and theoretician John Smith outlined a more stringent approach to the art of folding paper that he termed *Pureland*. The building blocks of origami are the valley fold and the mountain fold, which are often combined into more complex sequences that are executed simultaneously. Smith aimed to make origami more accessible by devising models that only use mountain folds and valley folds one at a time, as opposed to combinations of folds. This collection of origami pieces follows the Pureland style, along with the additional constraint of requiring that they can be folded comfortably from six-inch (or fifteen-centimeter) squares.

Following the Pureland guidelines is not just for ease of folding, as resulting works often have an understated elegance. Many complex origami pieces try to conceal their humble paper origins, sometimes to the point of tricking you into thinking they are as real as the subject they are portraying. Pureland origami embraces the look of being folded, much like traditional paper folds do.

Interestingly, most traditional origami does not qualify as being Pureland and often contain folds that would place them at an intermediate difficulty level. There has been an effort to develop Pureland equivalent sequences for these more advanced folds, often resulting in a convoluted progression. These works were designed to be Pureland from the outset for less labored folding processes.

Some small challenges will be found while folding these pieces. Many of them rely on very specific landmarks (found through folding) that demand accuracy when forming. A few models will employ hidden folds, where you will be called on to fold a layer that is not at the surface. Even with these complexities, this compilation is regarded as being at a simple level by modern origami standards. So, the contents are arranged by alphabetical order. If you are looking for an easier piece to start with, the ones with fewer steps will fit the bill. The ones with longer sequences can be rendered easier by simply taking a break between a stretch of steps. Following the Pureland philosophy does result in some novel combinations of folds, so have fun making these origami models for yourself!

Paper & Materials

Picking the perfect paper for your origami project can range from fun to frustrating. There are many origami designs with well over a hundred steps that demand specialty papers that can handle their stressful folding sequences. Fortunately, all these simpler pieces can be made from almost any paper made for origami. While it might be tempting to just use copy paper (or any scrap paper lying around), often such materials are too thick to handle more than a few layers of folds.

One of the better varieties to consider is kami, which is the Japanese word for *paper*. It is often just simply sold as *origami paper*, being extremely common. It can be found on most online stores, hobby shops, and of course origami stores (such as The Source, which is part of OrigamiUSA). The standard size is six inches (or fifteen centimeters) which is suitable for these projects. You could also consider the larger ten-inch size (or twenty-five-centimeter variety).

Most kami papers sport a decorative side (either plain or patterned) with the other side being plain white. A few of the models showcase both sides of the paper, so you should consider the *duo* or *double-sided* variety of kami. Of course, stay clear from the papers that are simply the same color on both sides.

Other papers sold for origami purposes are not as easy to work with. Foil backed papers do look nice and shiny when they are pristine, but they will pick up any extraneous creases as you fold. Some sequences call for changing a valley fold to a mountain fold, and foil papers a notoriously inflexible at that task. Washi papers are typically very durable, but do not often hold a crease well without special treatment. One solution is to use glue while folding, with PVA adhesives being ideal.

More adventurous folders might consider custom paper preparations. This can be as simple as using a favorite giftwrap and cutting it down to size. If you are considering getting a paper cutter, rotary style is more accurate and far safer than the guillotine kind. A popular European wrapping paper variety is known as *kraft* paper, which is the German word for *strong*. Most origami shops will sell it precut into squares. Unfortunately, like most wrapping paper, it is plain on the other side. Some origami artists will paint their papers with watered down acrylic paints.

A less messy approach is to glue a lightweight sheet onto the other side. A perfect adhesive for this application is methylcellulose, often abbreviated as *MC*. MC comes in a powder form that needs to be mixed into cold water. About two teaspoons per 1.5 cups of water is a good ratio. After about thirty minutes of periodic stirring the MC will reach a syrupy consistency. It can be brushed on your paper (any cheap paintbrush is fine) after which you can place your thinner paper atop. You can then brush more MC for a better bond. The drying process can be accelerated with a table fan. Many of the models showcased here were prepared with this technique. Have fun experimenting with different materials.

Symbols & Terminology

Valley Fold is indicated by a dashed line: — — — — — — — —

It is typically accompanied with an open-headed arrow:

When you see this line style with this arrow, you need to fold forward in the direction of the arrow. Here is an example:

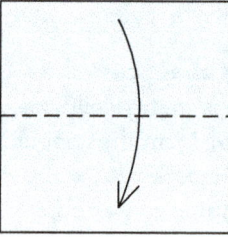 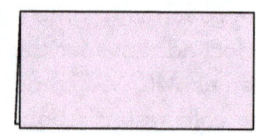

1. Valley fold in half.   2. Completed *Valley Fold.*

Although it is indicated to fold the top edge to the bottom edge, it typically physically easier to fold in the direction away from your body. So, when folding you will often rotate your model to what is comfortable and then return to the orientation indicated in the diagrams.

Also note in these examples (and for all of the illustrations throughout) you need to look at both the current step and the subsequent step. The current step informs you on what you are supposed to do. The next step will show you the results of what you need to do, and makes following the directions much clearer.

Mountain fold is indicated by a dashed line with dots: —·—·—·—·—·—·

It is typically accompanied with a closed-headed arrow:

When you see this line style with this arrow, you need to fold behind in the direction of the arrow. Here is an example:

1. Mountain fold in half.   2. Completed *Mountain Fold*.

To accomplish this, you will often turn your model over and form a valley fold. You would then turn your model back over. So in a sense the mountain fold is a shorthand approach to avoid having many diagrams show your model being flipped over a number of times.

Precrease is indicated by a dashed (valley fold) line: — — — — — — —

It is typically accompanied with a double-headed arrow (one side open and the other closed):

Once completed, it is indicated by a thin solid line that does not extend to the edge of the paper: ———————— Here is an example:

1. Precrease in half.   2. Completed *Precrease*.

To accomplish this, you first form a valley fold (in the direction of the open arrowhead) and then open out the paper (in the direction of the closed arrowhead).

Precrease with a Mountain Fold is indicated by a mountain fold line: —‑—‑—‑—‑—‑—‑

It is typically accompanied with a double-headed arrow (one side open and the other half open):

Once completed, it is indicated by a thin solid line that does not extend to the edge of the paper: ——————— Here is an example:

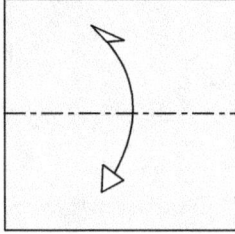 

1. Precrease in half with a mountain fold.
2. Completed *Precrease*.

To accomplish this, you first form a mountain fold (in the direction of the half open arrowhead) and then open out the paper (in the direction of the open arrowhead).

Pleat Fold is indicated by a mountain fold line followed by a valley fold line. An arrow indicates the direction of the pleat. Here is an example:

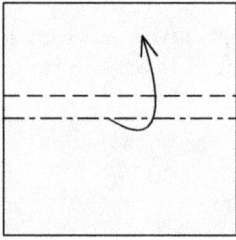 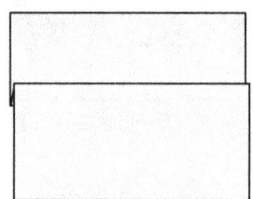

1. Pleat fold upwards.
2. Completed *Pleat Fold*.

To accomplish this, you first form the mountain fold and pull that folded edge into position. Flattening this will create the pleat (creating a zigzag formation).

Hidden/Imaginary lines are indicated by a thin dotted line: ----------

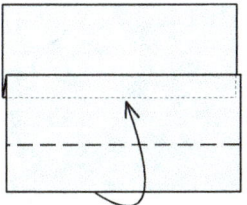 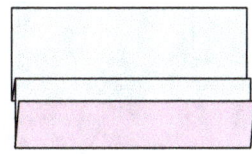

1. Valley fold to the hidden edge.

2. Completed fold.

Dots are sometimes used to call attention to a specific landmark:

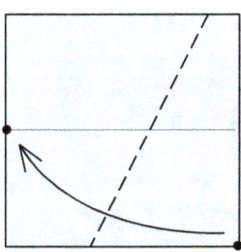 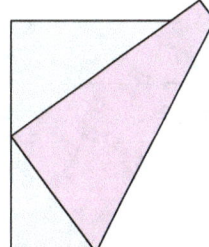

1. Valley fold the dotted corner to the dotted crease.

2. Completed fold.

Open dots are sometimes used to indicate angle bisectors.

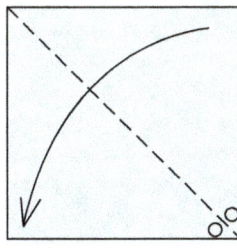 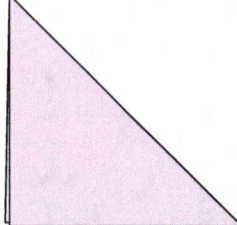

1. Valley fold along the indicated angle bisector.

2. Completed fold.

11

Turn over is indicated by a looped arrow:

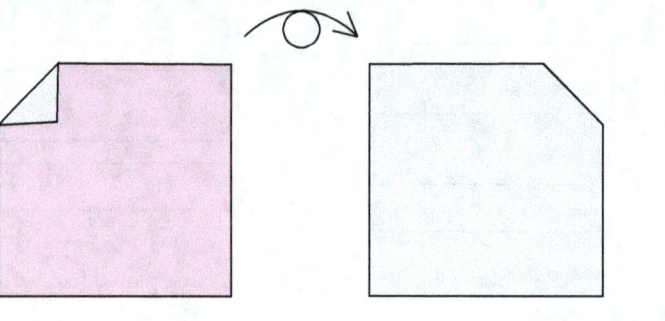

Rotate is indicated by a circle with arrows along it:

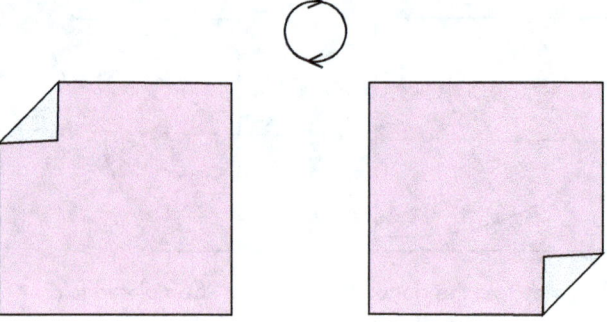

Angel

angel

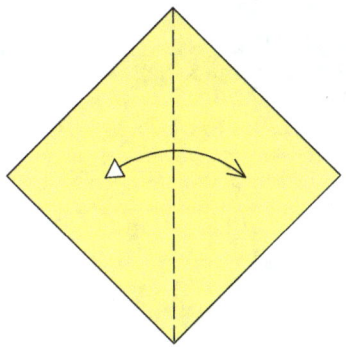

1. Precrease along the diagonal.

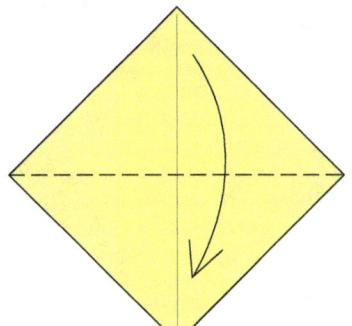

2. Valley fold in half.

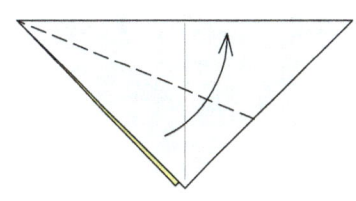

3. Valley fold the top layer up.

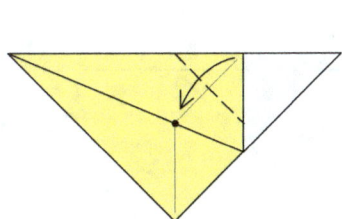

4. Valley fold the corner to the dotted intersection.

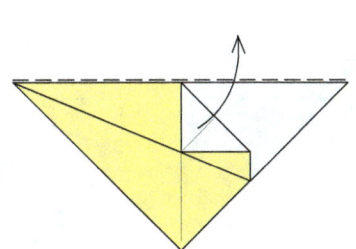

5. Unfold everything but the last fold.

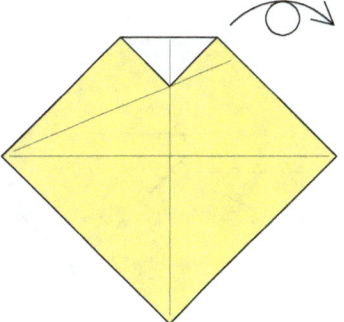

6. Turn over.

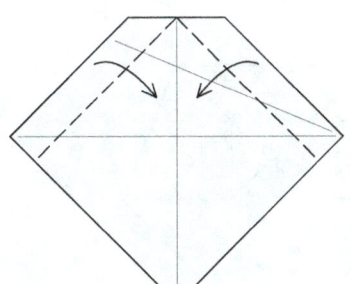

7. Valley fold the sides inward.

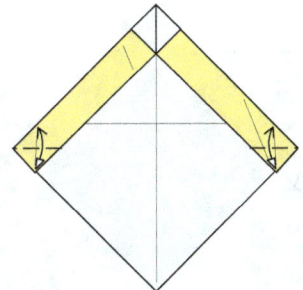

8. Precrease the top layer at each side.

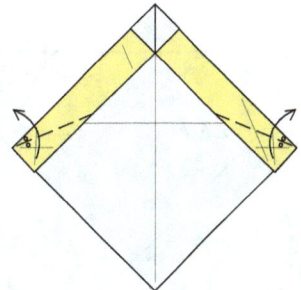

9. Valley fold along the indicated angle bisectors.

angel

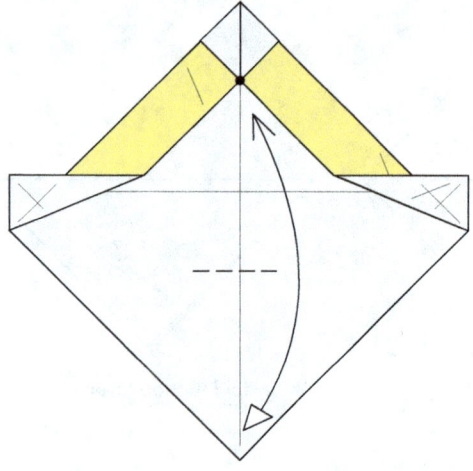

10. Precrease partway to the dotted intersection.

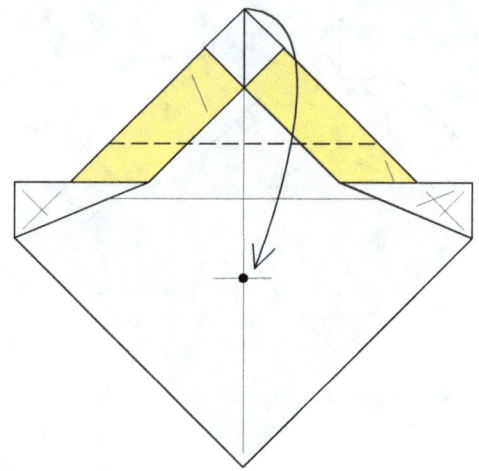

11. Valley fold to the dotted intersection.

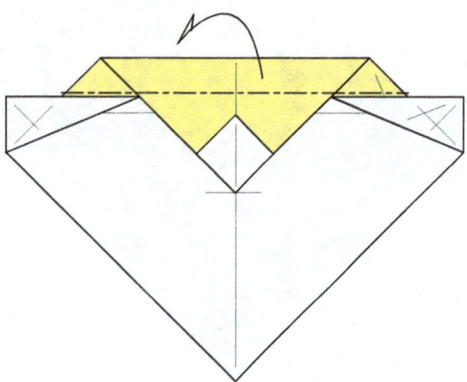

12. Mountain fold the edge behind.

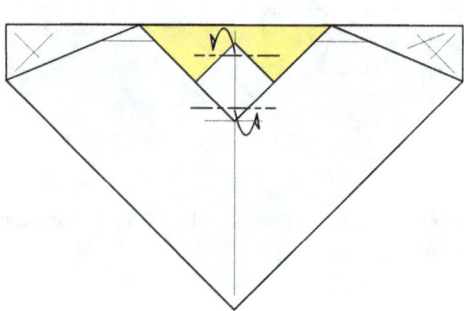

13. Mountain fold the corners. There are no reference points for these folds.

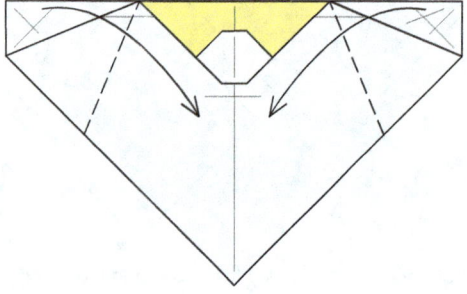

14. Valley fold to the center.

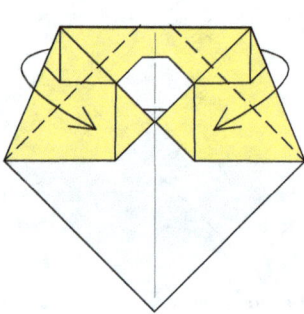

15. Valley fold the sides.

angel

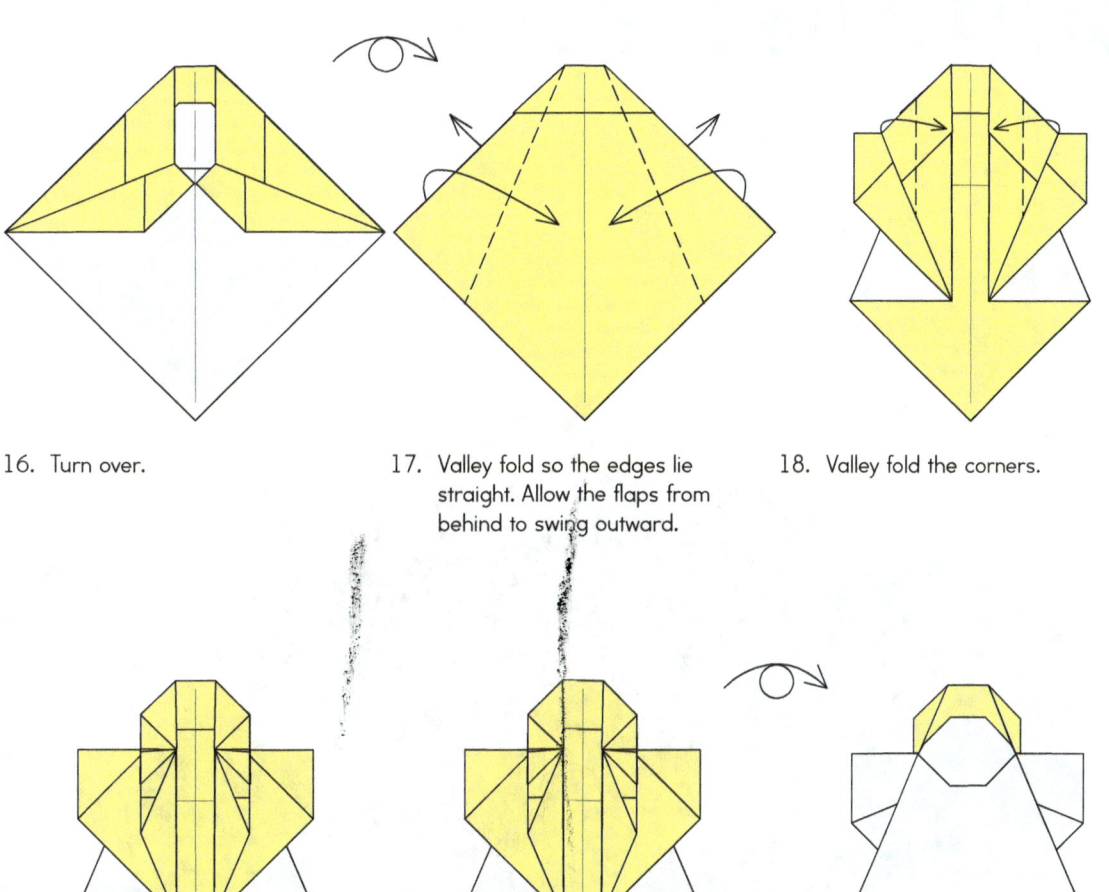

16. Turn over.

17. Valley fold so the edges lie straight. Allow the flaps from behind to swing outward.

18. Valley fold the corners.

19. Valley fold to the imaginary dotted intersection.

20. Turn over.

21. Completed *Angel*.

Bumblebee

bumblebee

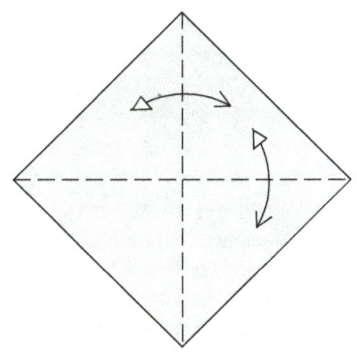

1. Precrease in half along the diagonals.

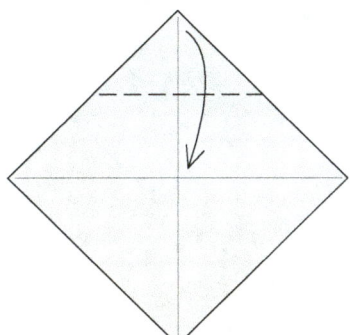

2. Valley fold the top corner to the center.

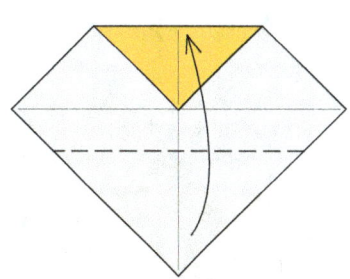

3. Valley fold the bottom corner up to the top edge.

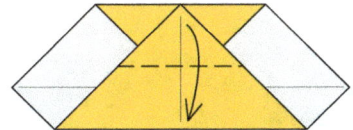

4. Valley fold the corner down to the bottom edge.

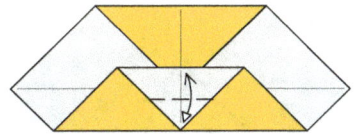

5. Precrease the triangular flap in half.

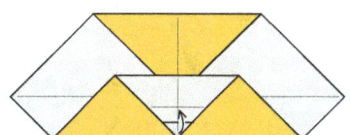

6. Valley fold the corner to the last crease.

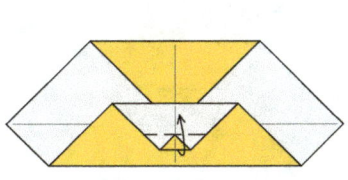

7. Valley fold up along the existing crease.

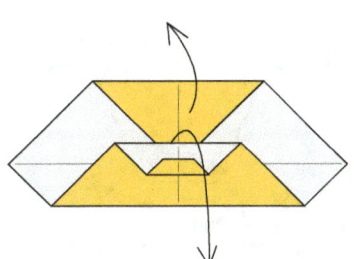

8. Open out the two flaps.

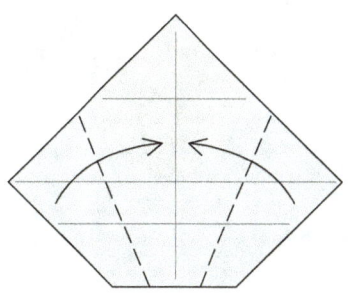

9. Valley fold the sides to the center.

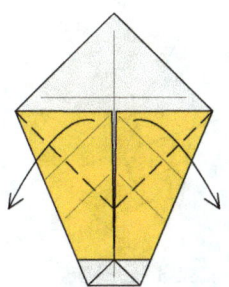

10. Valley fold the flaps outwards, keeping the side edges straight.

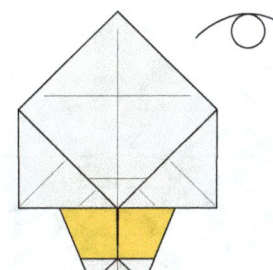

11. Turn over.

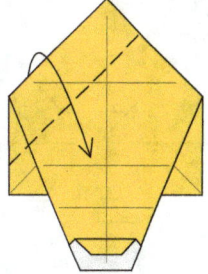

12. Valley fold towards the indicated crease.

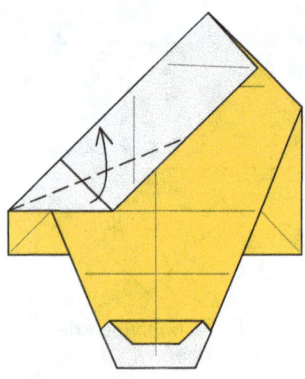
13. Valley fold to the top edge.

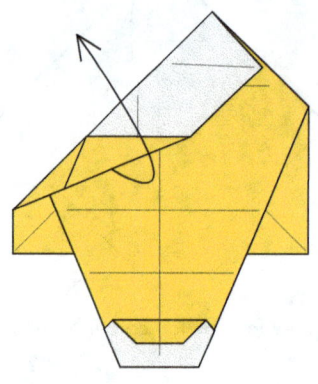
14. Open out the flap.

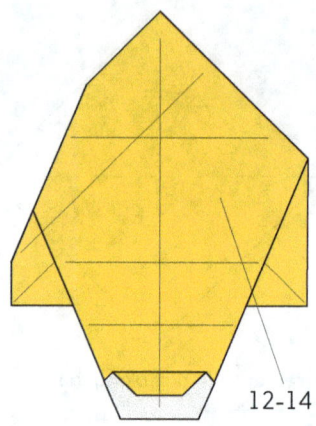
15. Repeat steps 12-14 in mirror image.

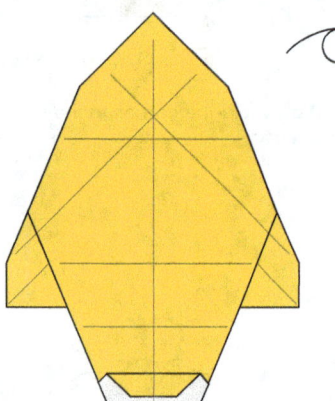
16. Turn over.

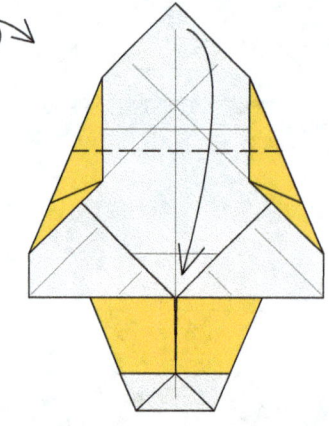
17. Valley fold the corner down to the intersection of folds.

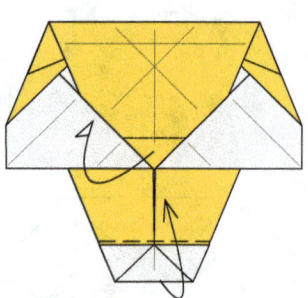
18. Valley fold the tip of the flap behind. Valley fold the lower edge up.

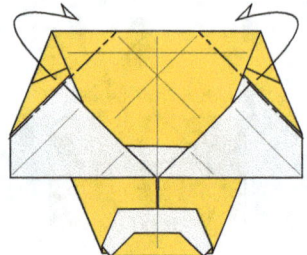
19. Mountain fold the top corners behind.

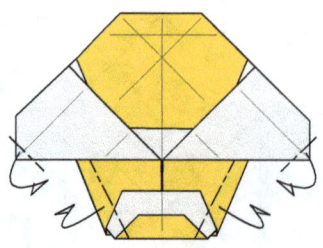
20. Mountain fold the edges of the tail behind. Mountain fold the corners of the wings behind.

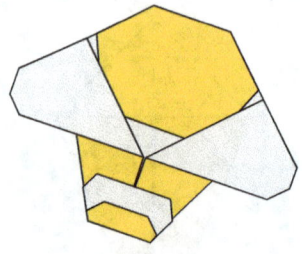
21. Completed *Bumblebee*.

Butterfly

butterfly

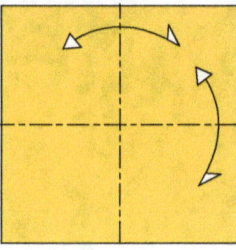

1. Precrease the sides with mountain folds.

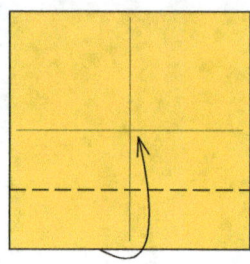

2. Valley fold the bottom edge to the center.

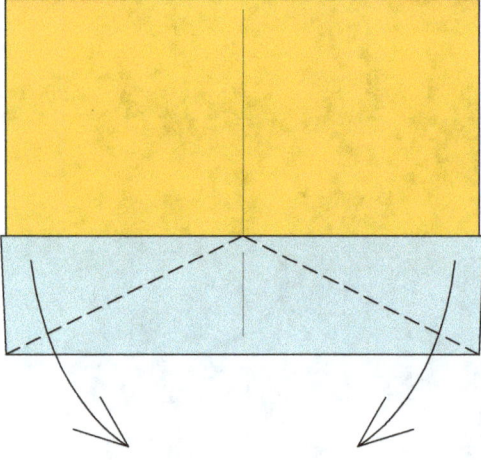

3. Valley fold the corners down.

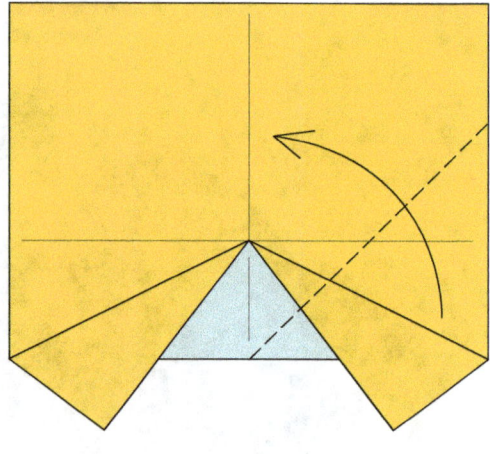

4. Valley fold the bottom edge to lie along the center.

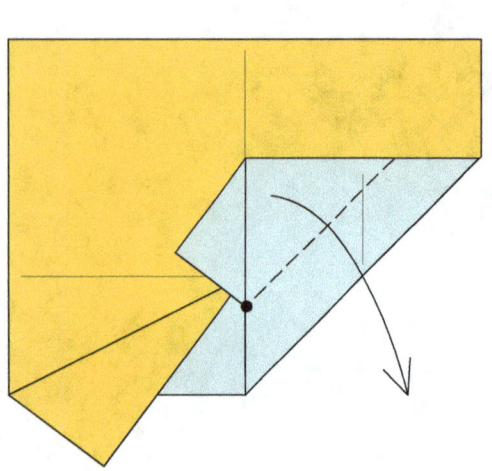

5. Starting from the dotted corner valley fold down. The resulting side edge should lie straight.

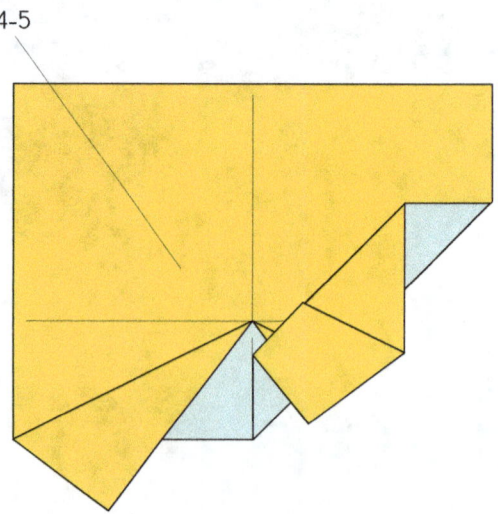

4-5

6. Repeat steps 4-5 in mirror image.

butterfly

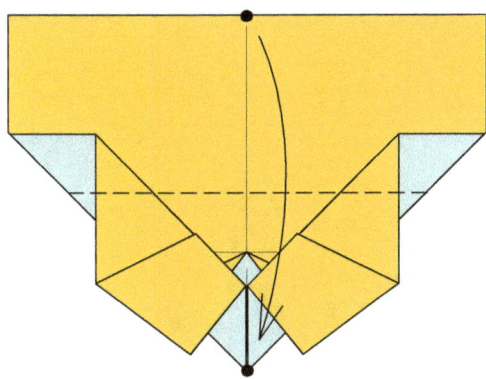

7. Valley fold the dotted edge to the dotted corner.

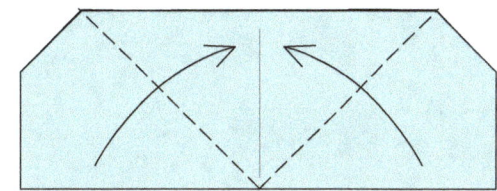

8. Valley fold the sides to the center.

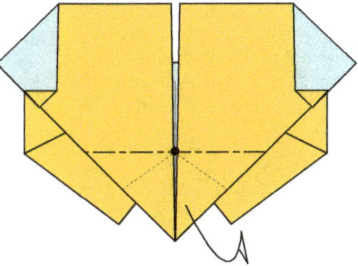

9. Mountain fold the corner inside starting from the hidden dotted corner.

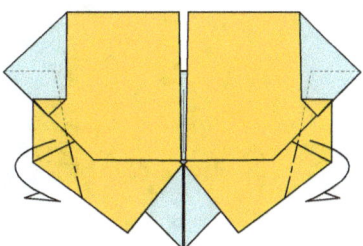

10. Mountain fold the sides inside to taste. Parts of the folds are hidden.

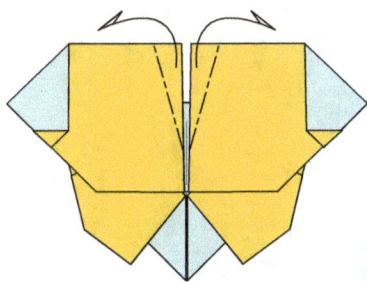

11. Mountain fold the corners inside to taste.

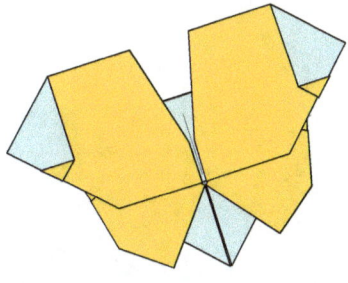

12. Completed *Butterfly*.

23

Calla Lily

calla lily

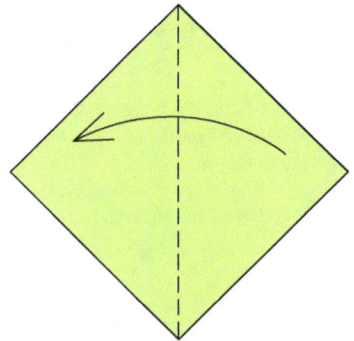

1. Valley fold along the diagonal.

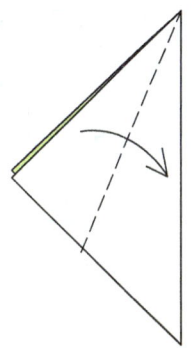

2. Valley fold along the angle bisector.

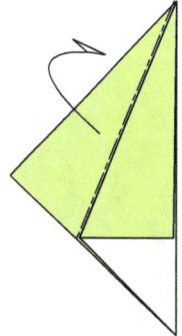

3. Mountain fold the back layer to match the front.

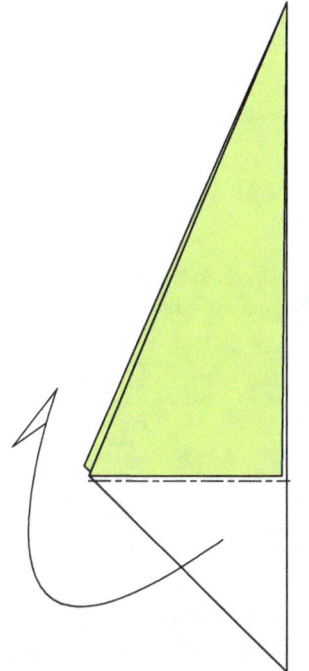

4. Mountain fold the bottom triangle.

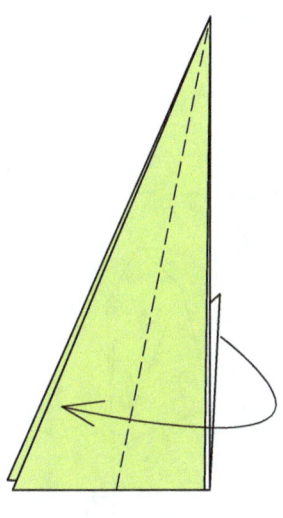

5. Valley fold all of the layers along the angle bisector.

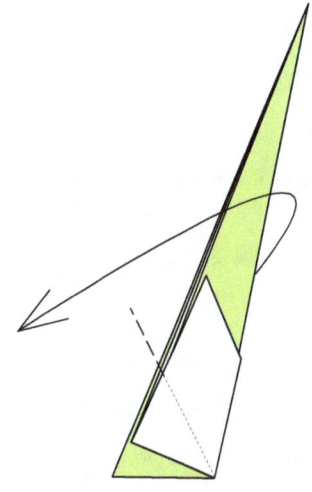

6. Valley fold the long flap along the angle bisector. The fold is hidden under the top layer.

calla lily

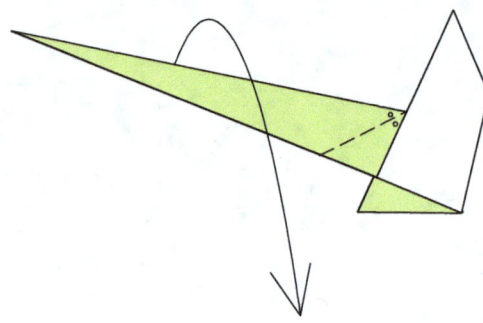

7. Valley fold along the angle bisector.

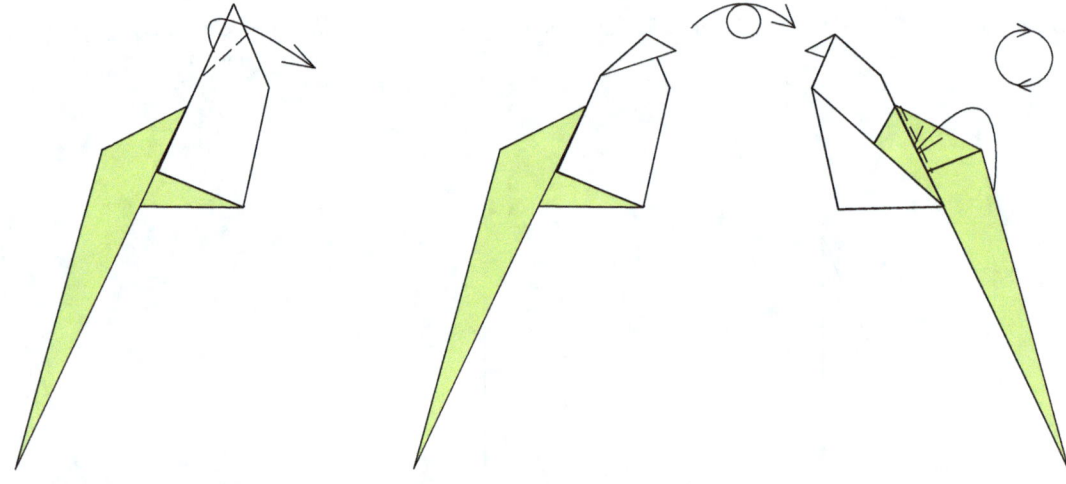

8. Valley fold the tip. There are no reference points for this fold.

9. Turn over.

10. Tuck the long flap inside. Rotate the model slightly.

Car

car

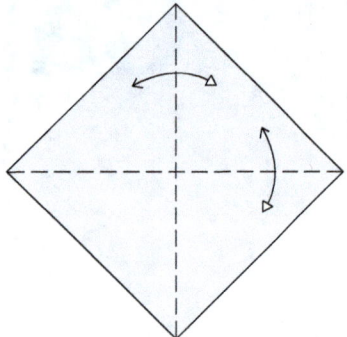

1. Precrease along the diagonals.

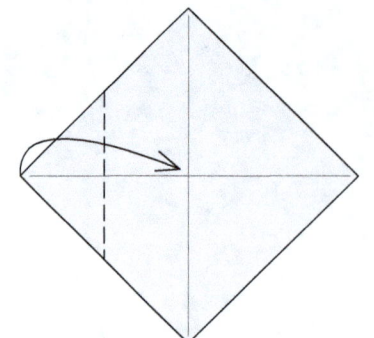

2. Valley fold to the center.

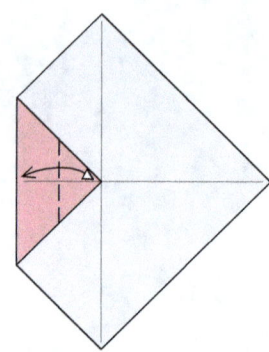

3. Precrease the flap in half.

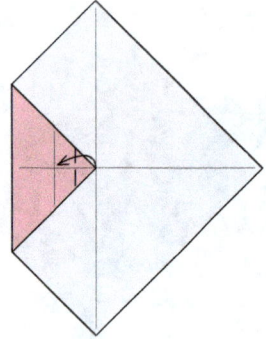

4. Valley fold the corner to the crease.

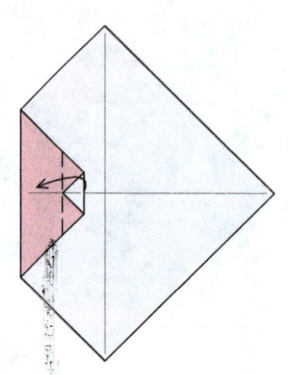

5. Valley fold along the existing crease.

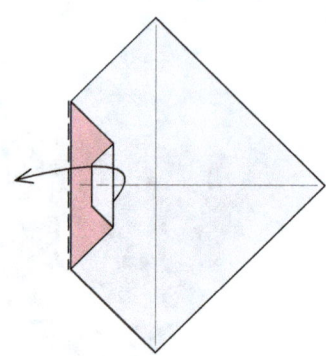

6. Swing the flap over.

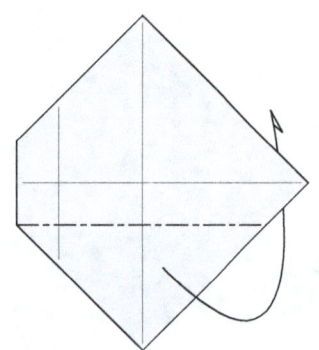

7. Mountain fold starting from the left corner.

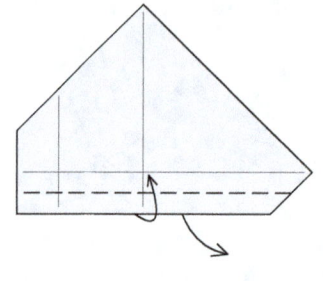

8. Valley fold to the center, allowing the flap from behind to swing forward.

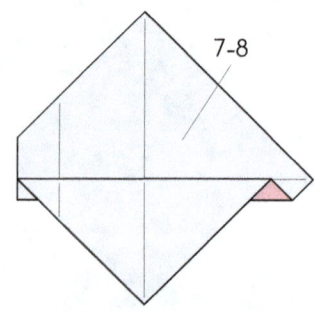

9. Repeat steps 7-8 at the top.

car

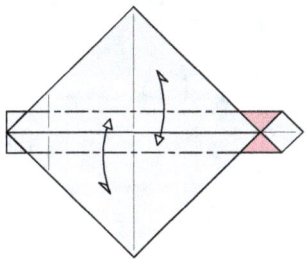

10. Precrease along the hidden edges with mountain folds.

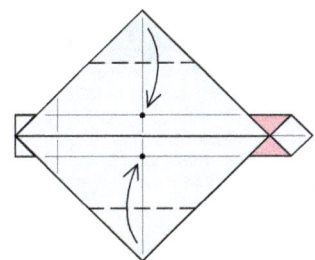

11. Valley fold the corners to the dotted intersections of creases.

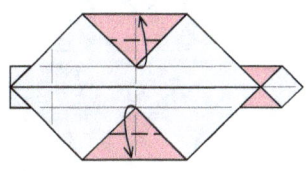

12. Valley fold the corners to the outer edges.

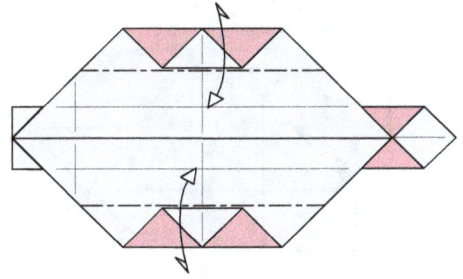

13. Precrease with mountain folds.

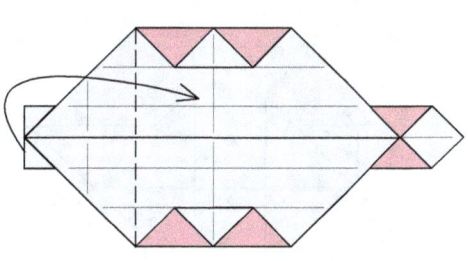

14. Valley fold the side inwards.

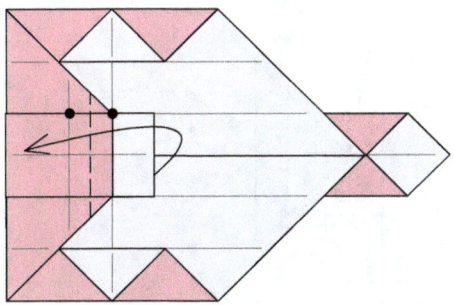

15. Valley fold so the dotted sections meet.

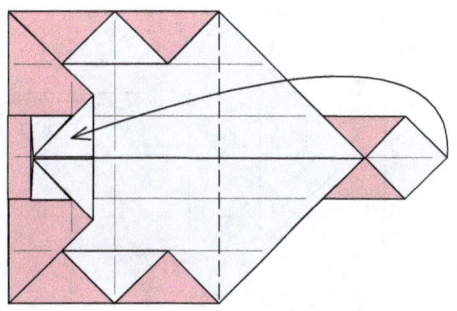

16. Valley fold the other side over.

car

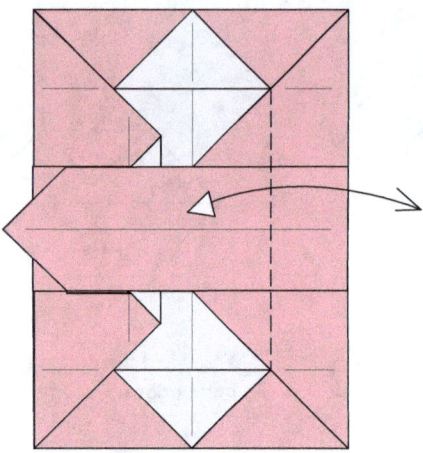

17. Precrease the top flap.

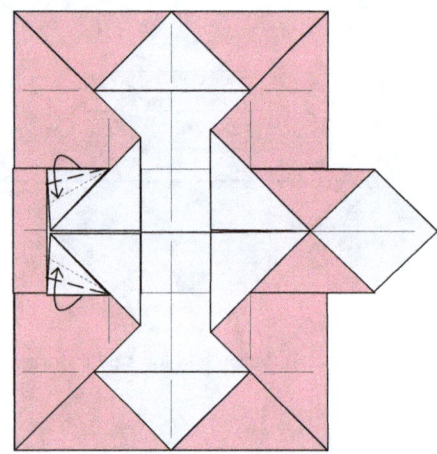

18. Valley fold so the dotted sections meet.

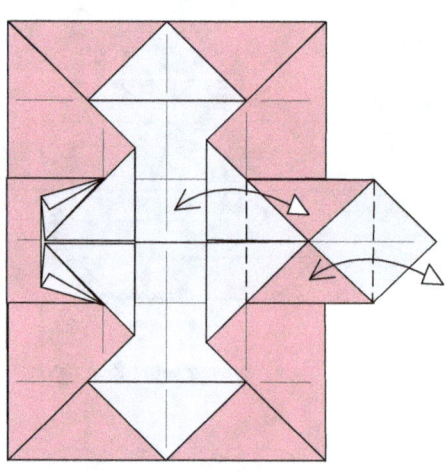

19. Valley fold the sides inwards along angle trisectors.

20. Precrease the top flap along the indicated sections.

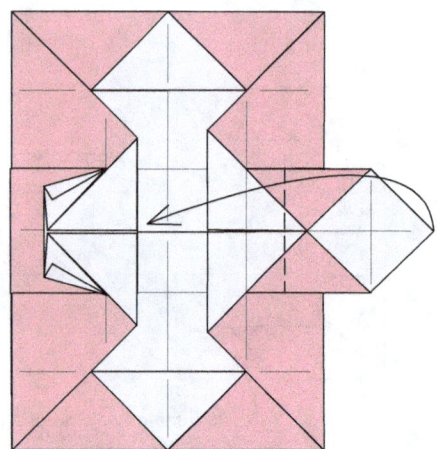

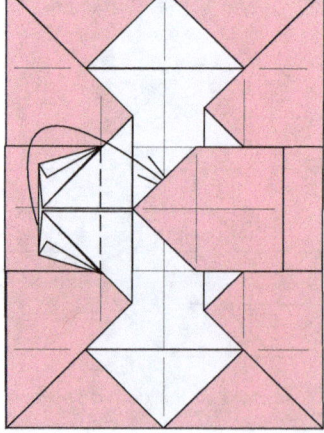

21. Valley fold the corner to the edge.

22. Valley fold under the right flap.

30

car

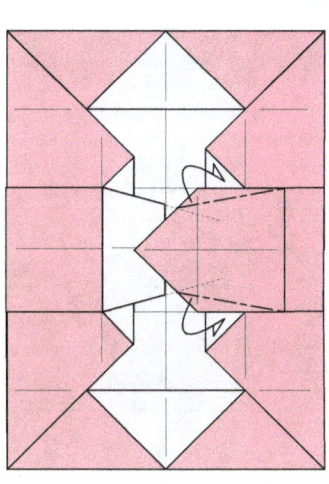
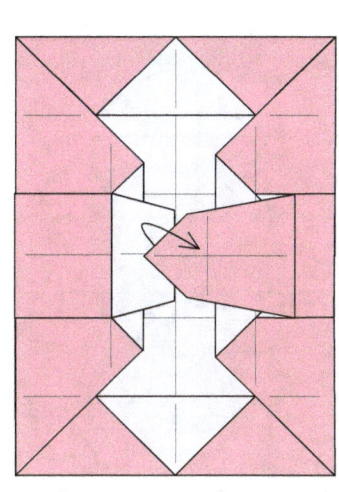
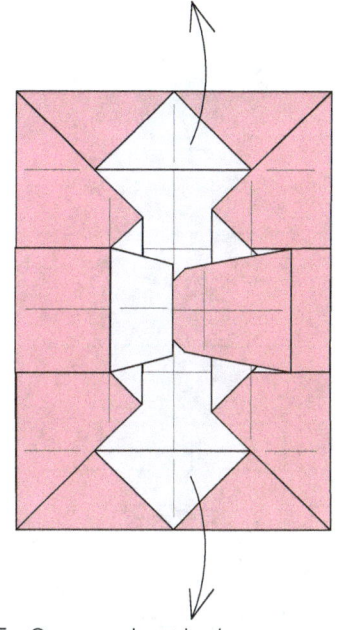

23. Mountain fold the sides so they intersect with the imaginary continuation of edges of the flap at the left.

24. Tuck the flap into the pocket.

25. Open out the side pleats.

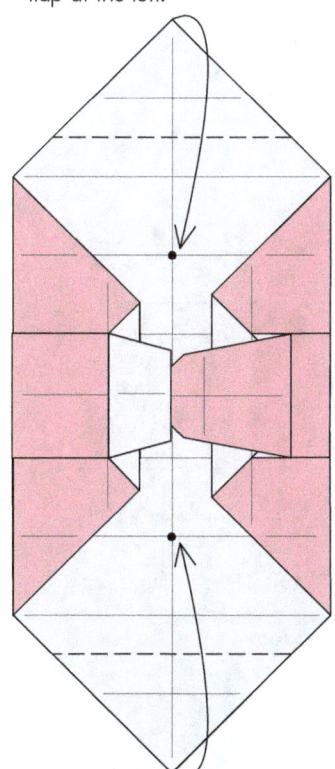
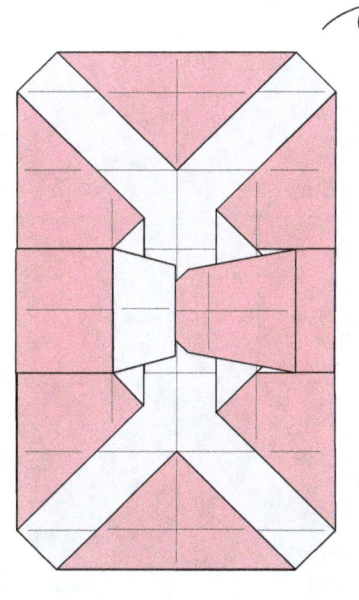

26. Valley fold the corners to the dotted intersection of creases.

27. Turn over.

28. Valley fold the corners to the creases.

31

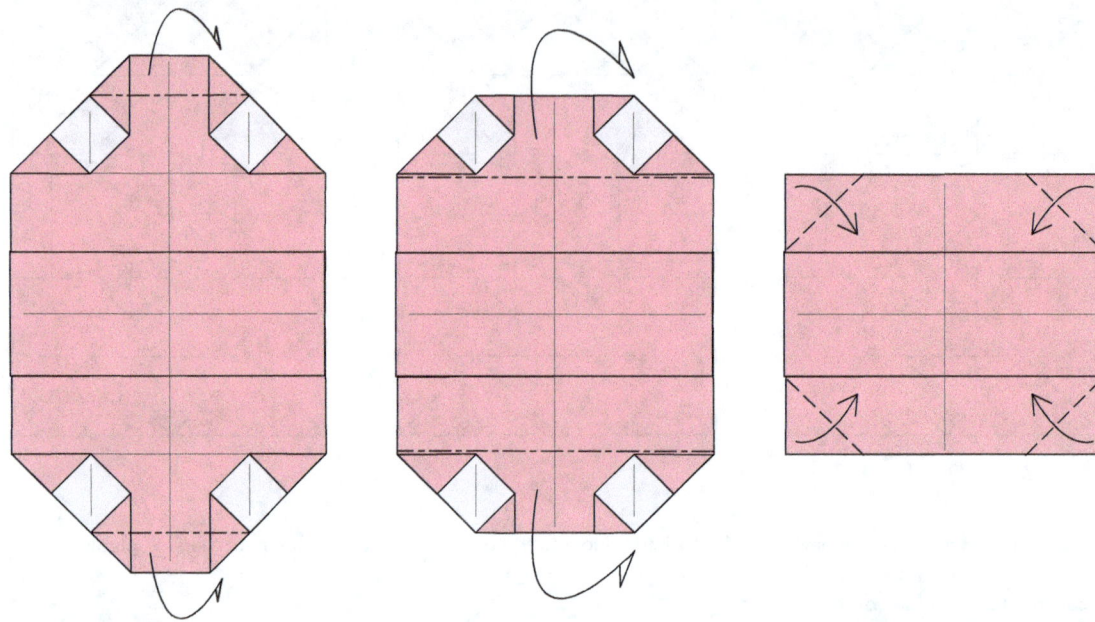

29. Mountain fold the sides.

30. Mountain fold the sides.

31. Valley fold the four corners inwards.

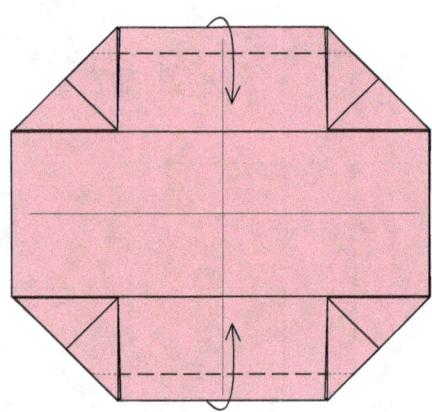

32. Valley fold the sides inwards at about 1/4 the width. Parts of the folds are hidden.

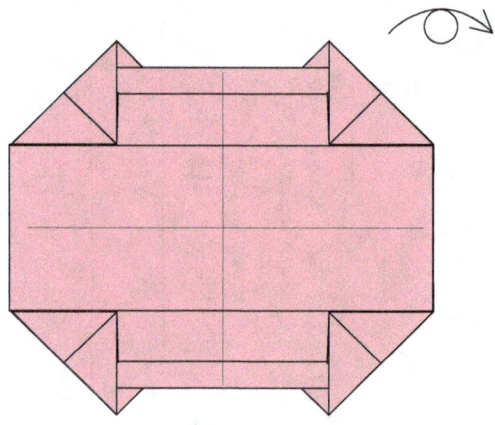

33. Turn over.

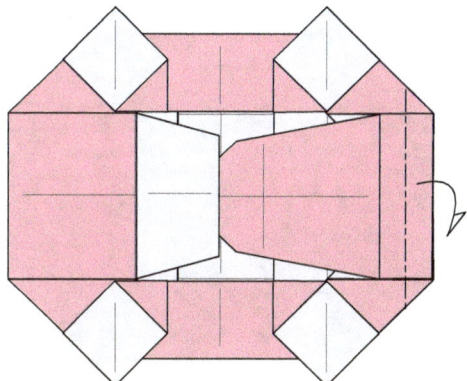
34. Mountain fold the edge behind.

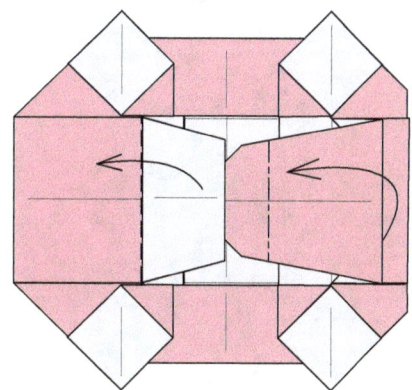
35. Raise the flaps up into a 3-D formation while inserting the right flap further into the left section.

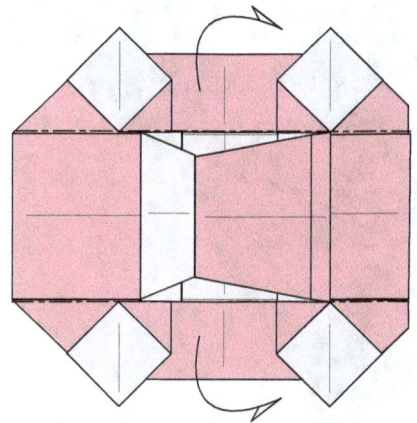
36. Mountain fold the sides at 90 degree angles.

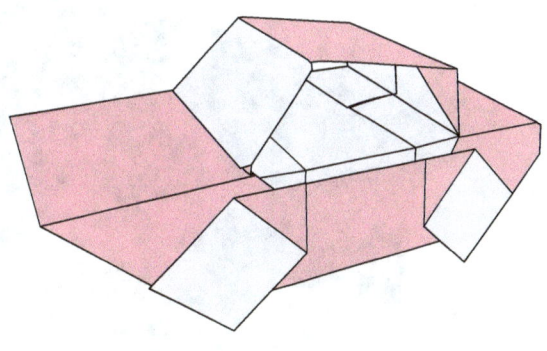
37. Completed *Car*.

Dachshund

dachshund

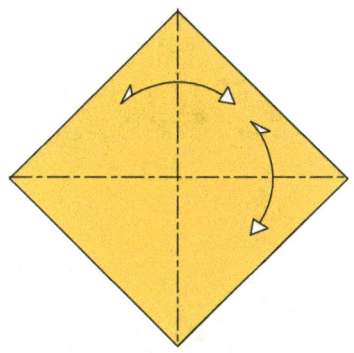
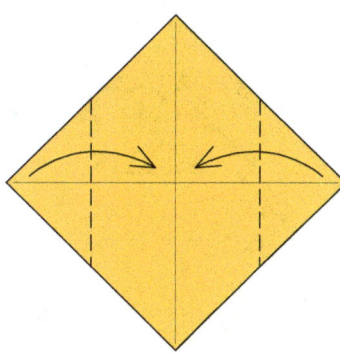
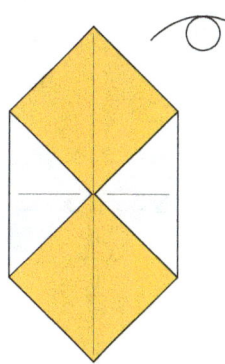

1. Precrease the diagonals with mountain folds.

2. Valley fold the corners to the center.

3. Turn over.

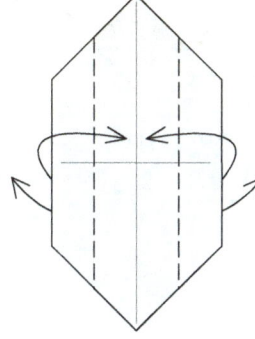
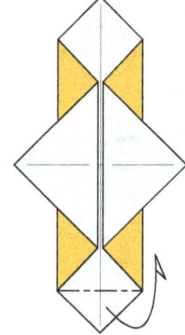
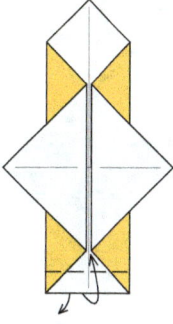

4. Valley fold the sides to the center, allowing the flaps from behind to swing forward.

5. Mountain fold.

6. Valley fold the edge up, allowing the flap from behind to swing forward.

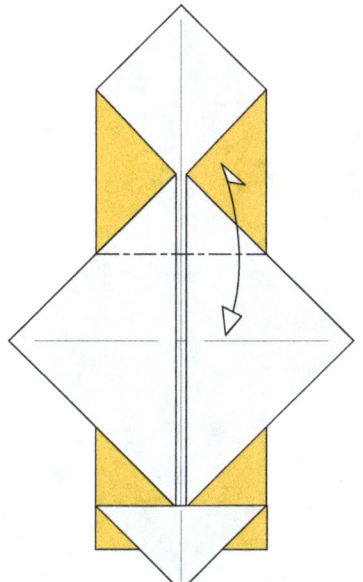
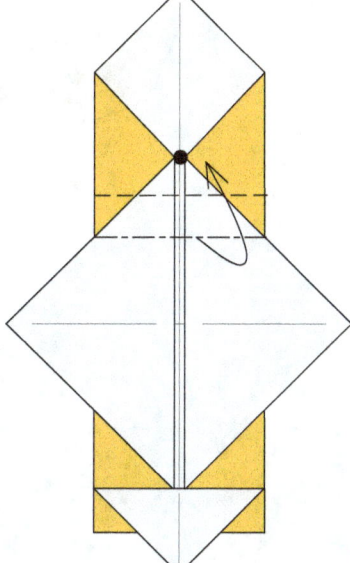
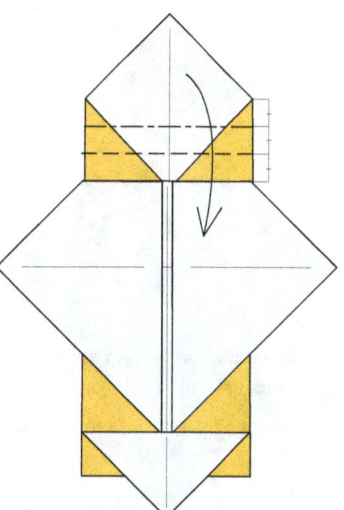

7. Precrease with a mountain fold.

8. Form a pleat by bringing the last crease towards the dotted intersection.

9. Pleat the top section into thirds.

dachshund

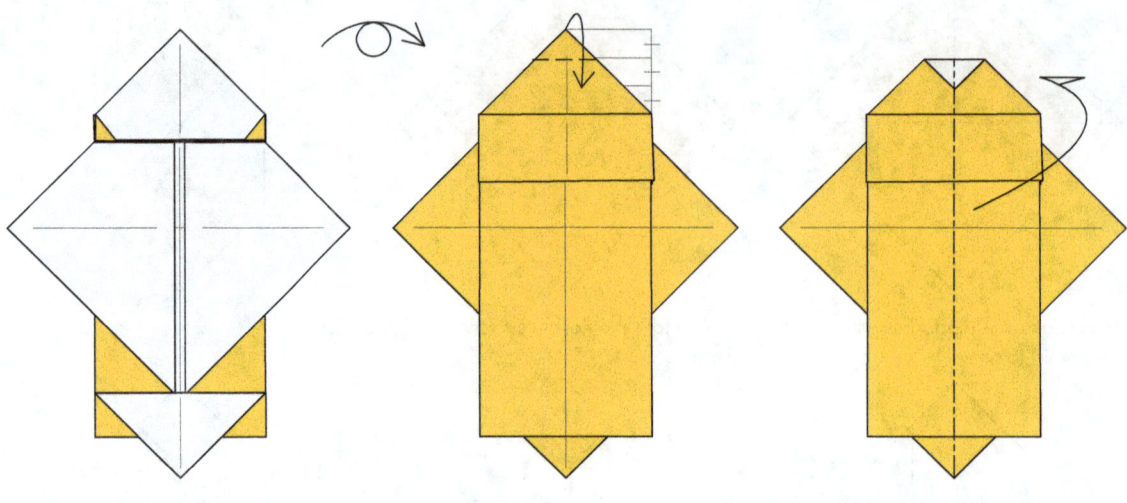

10. Turn over.

11. Valley fold the tip in.

12. Mountain fold in half.

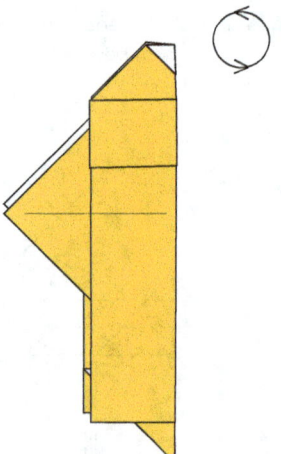

13. Rotate the model and spread it apart slightly so it stands.

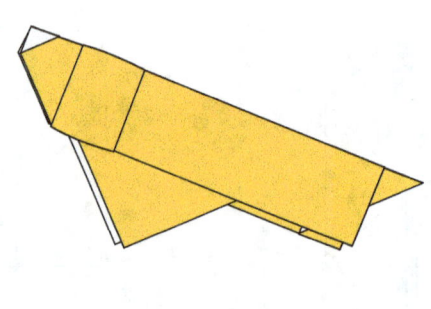

14. Completed *Dachshund*.

Dragon

dragon

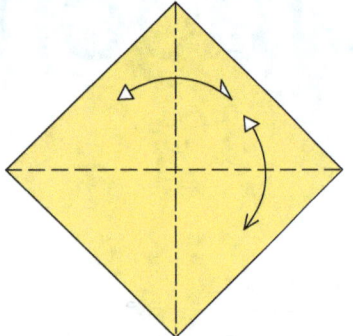

1. Precrease the diagonals with a valley fold and a mountain fold.

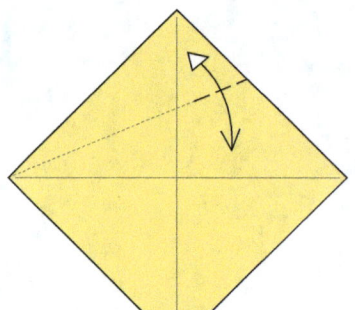

2. Precrease along the angle bisector, only creasing by the edge.

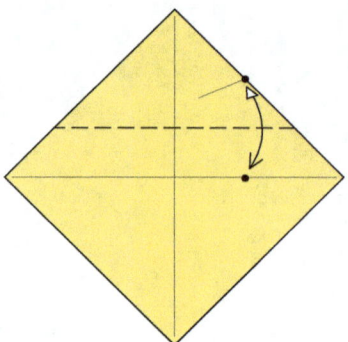

3. Precrease between the dotted sections.

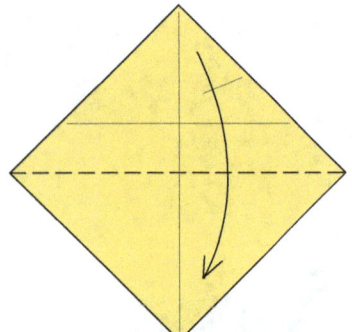

4. Valley fold along the center.

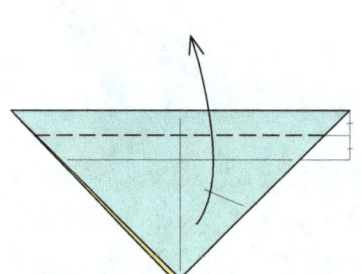

5. Valley fold up, dividing the indicated section in half.

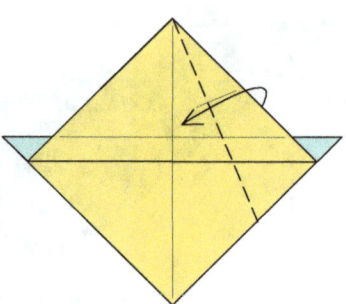

6. Valley fold along the angle bisector.

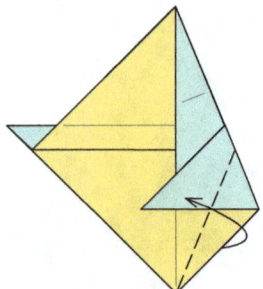

7. Valley fold along the angle bisector.

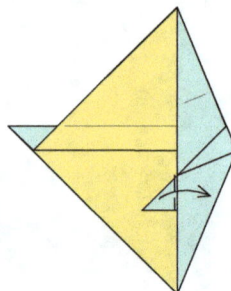

8. Valley fold the flap over.

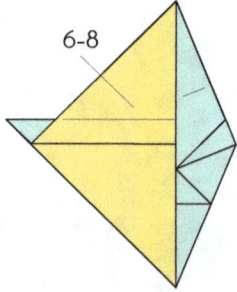

9. Repeat steps 6-8 in mirror image.

dragon

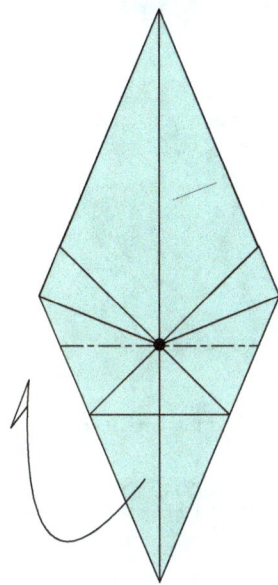
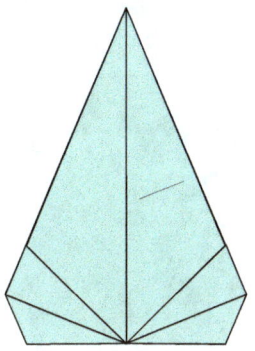
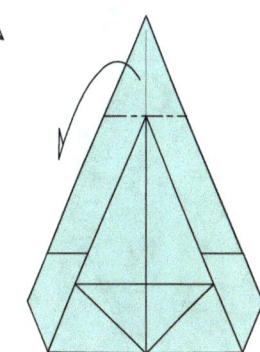

10. Mountain fold using the dotted intersection.

11. Turn over.

12. Mountain fold the rear flap.

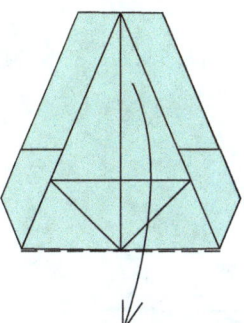
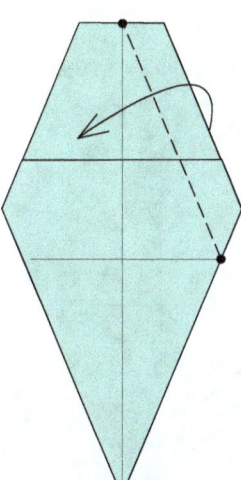
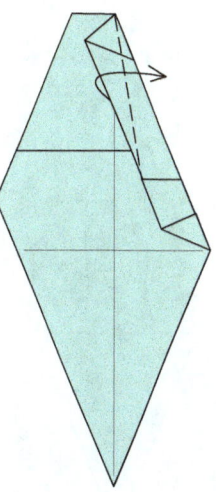

13. Swing the front flap down.

14. Valley fold between the dotted intersections.

15. Valley fold the edge outwards.

39

dragon

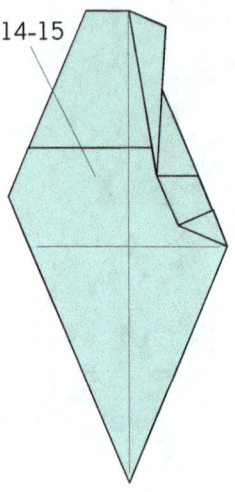
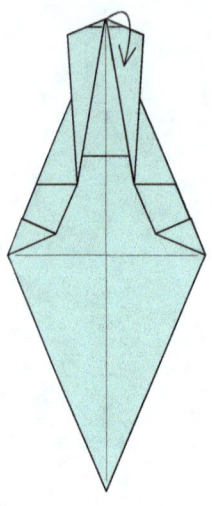
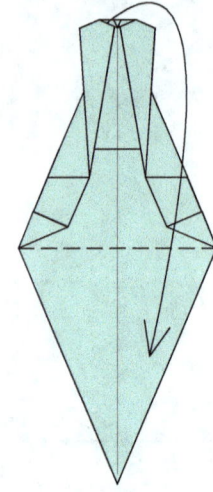

16. Repeat steps 14-15 in mirror image.

17. Valley fold a little bit of the tip of the flap.

18. Valley fold the flap down.

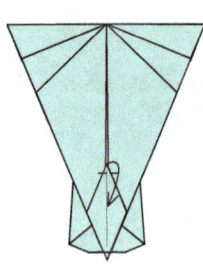
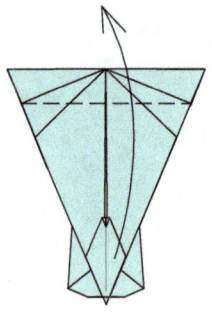
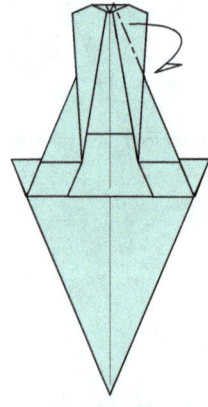

19. Valley fold a little bit of the tip of the flap.

20. Valley fold the flap up.

21. Mountain fold one of the flaps around.

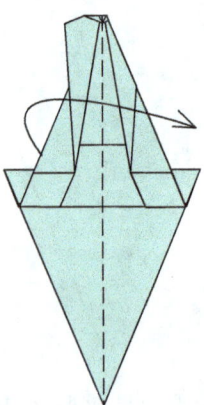
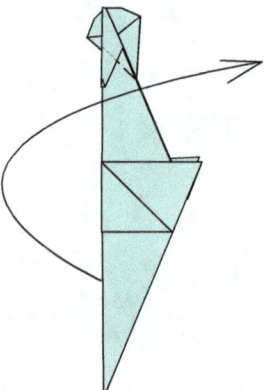
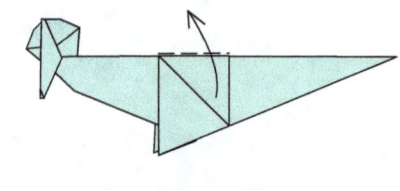

22. Valley fold in half.

23. Valley fold the body section over. Part of the fold is hidden under the layers of the head.

24. Swing the flap up.

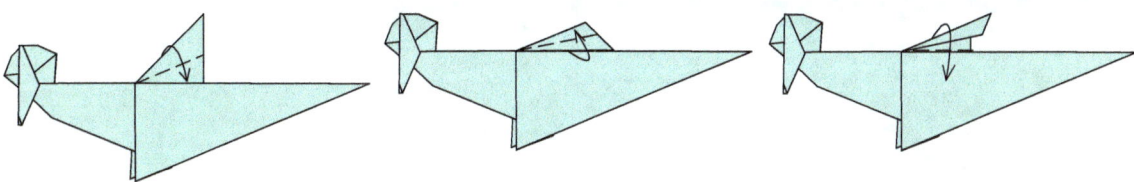

25. Valley fold along the angle bisection.

26. Valley fold along the angle bisection.

27. Swing the flap back down.

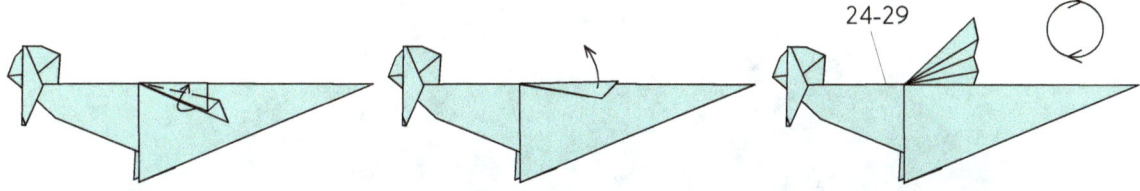

28. Valley fold along the angle bisection.

29. Spread open the pleats partway.

30. Repeat steps 24–29 behind. Rotate the model slightly.

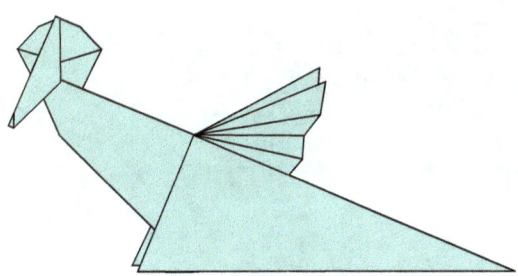

31. Completed *Dragon*.

Elephant

elephant

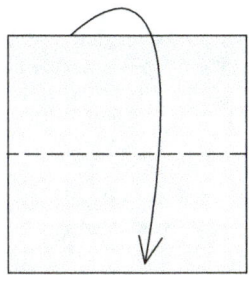

1. Valley fold the top edge down to the bottom.

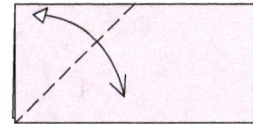

2. Lightly precrease the left side.

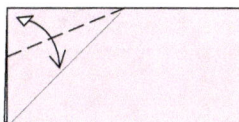

3. Lightly precrease along the angle bisector.

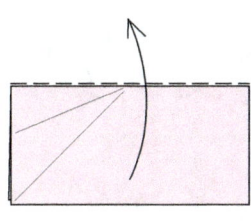

4. Open out.

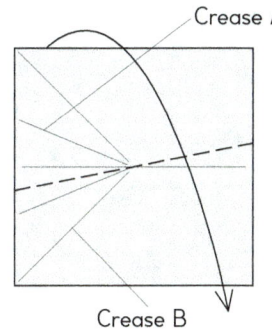

5. Valley fold so that crease A lies along crease B.

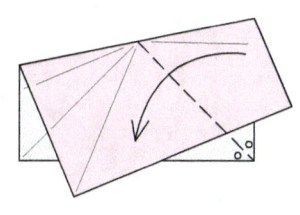

6. Valley fold along the indicated angle bisector.

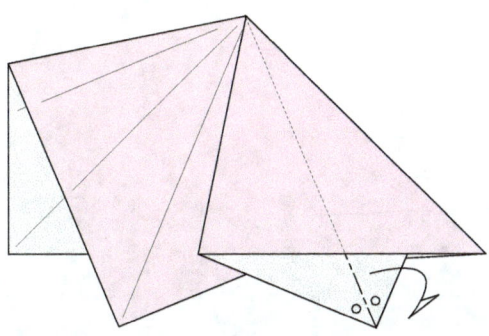

7. Mountain fold along the indicated angle bisector. Part of the fold is hidden.

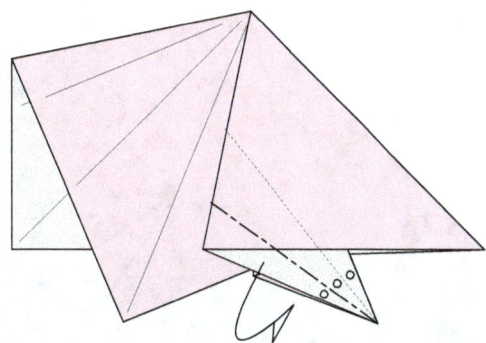

8. Mountain fold the edge in along the indicated angle trisector (a suggested reference point)

elephant

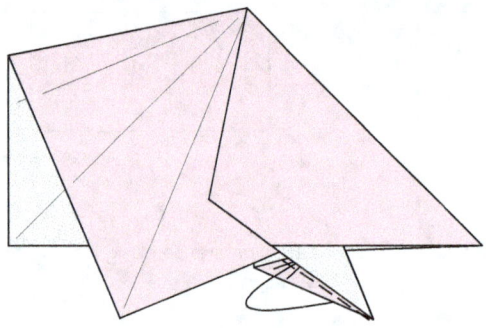

9. Valley fold the edge in to match the top layer.

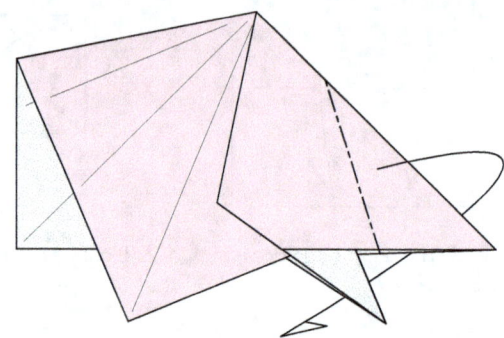

10. Mountain fold the corner behind. There are no reference points for this fold.

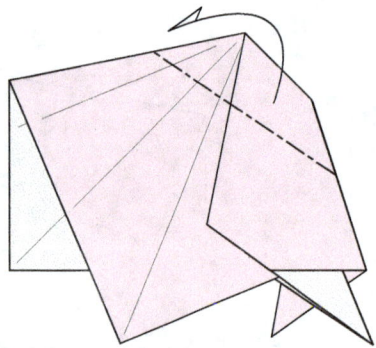

11. Mountain fold the edge behind. There are no reference points for this fold.

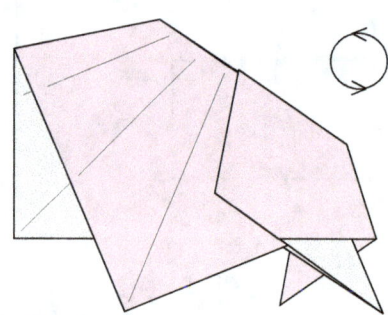

12. Rotate the model slightly.

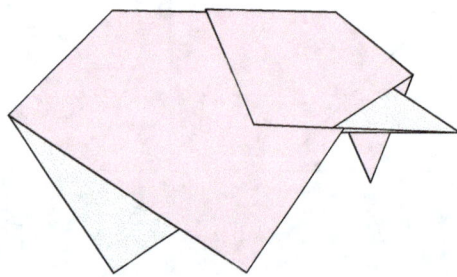

13. Completed *Elephant*.

Fish

f i s h

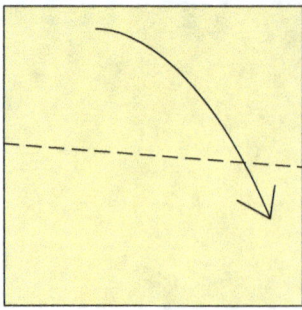

1. Make a slightly offset valley fold.

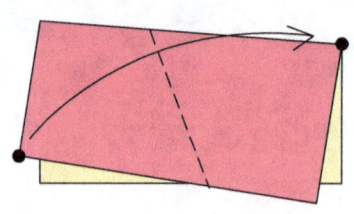

2. Valley fold such that the indicated corners meet.

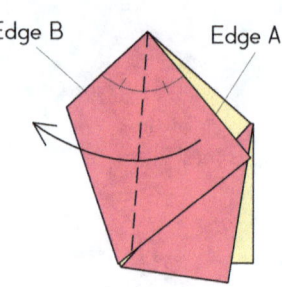

3. Valley fold the top layer along its angle bisector. Edge A will meet edge B.

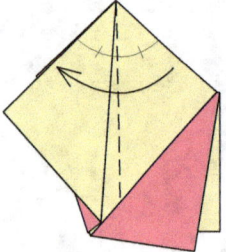

4. Valley fold the flap over so it meets the cluster of edges.

5. Turn over and rotate slightly.

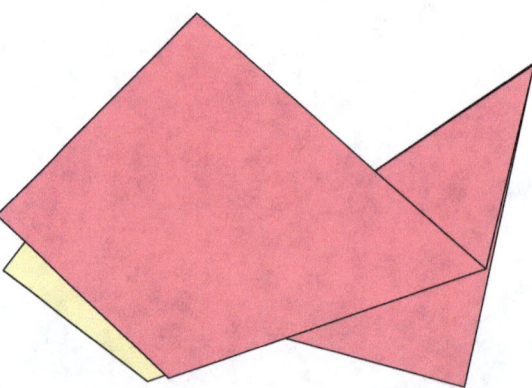

6. Completed *Fish*.

Frog

frog

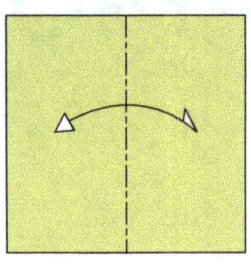

1. Precrease in half with a mountain folds.

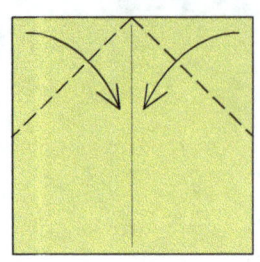

2. Valley fold to the center crease.

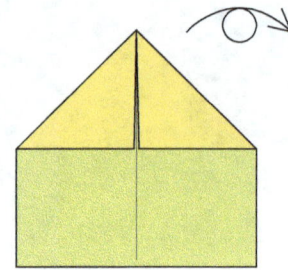

3. Turn over.

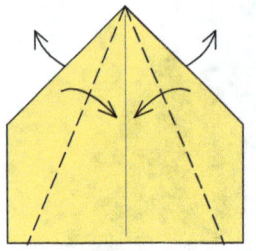

4. Valley fold to the center, allowing the flaps from behind to swing forward.

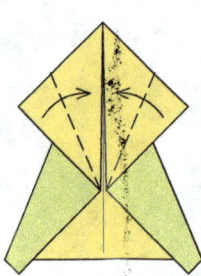

5. Valley fold the top flaps to the center.

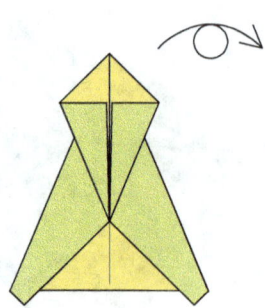

6. Turn over.

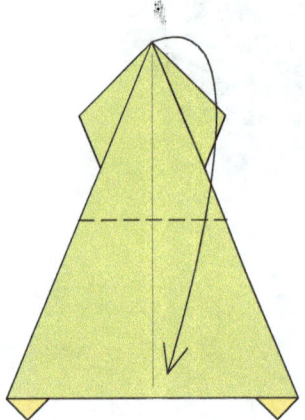

7. Valley fold to the bottom edge.

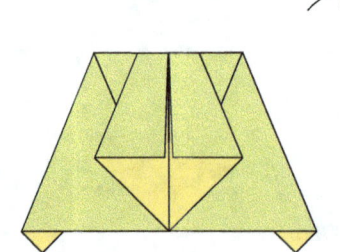

8. Turn over.

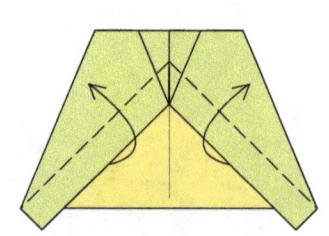

9. Valley fold the edges outwards.

frog

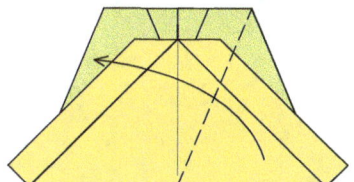

10. Starting from the center, valley fold the flap over.

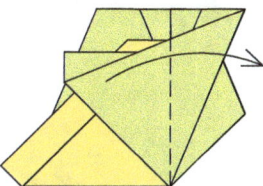

11. Valley fold the flap over along the center.

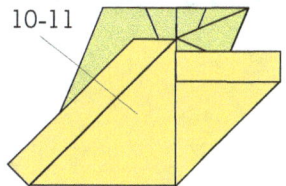

12. Repeat steps 10-11 in mirror image.

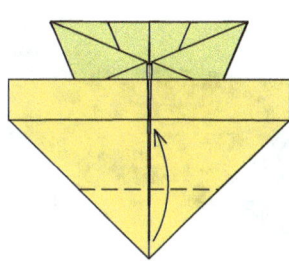

13. Valley fold up to the folded edges.

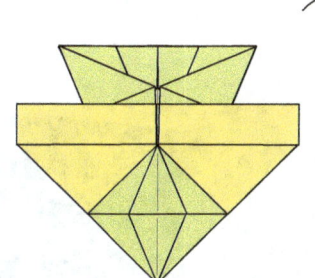

14. Turn over.

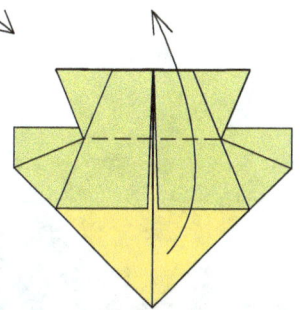

15. Valley fold the top flap up, starting from where the edges intersect.

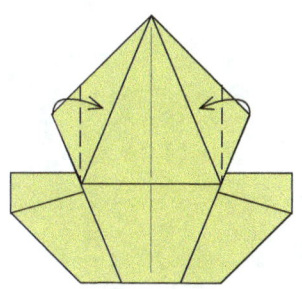

16. Valley fold the sides in.

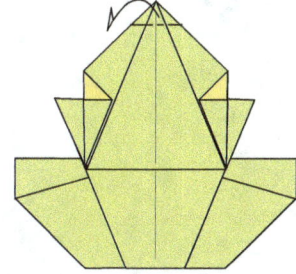

17. Mountain fold a little bit of the tip in.

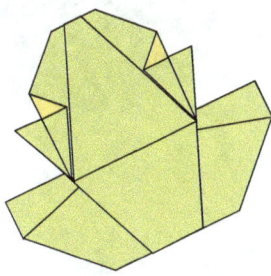

18. Completed *Frog*.

49

Guitar

guitar

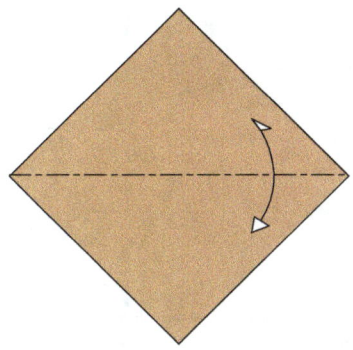

1. Precrease along the diagonal with a mountain fold.

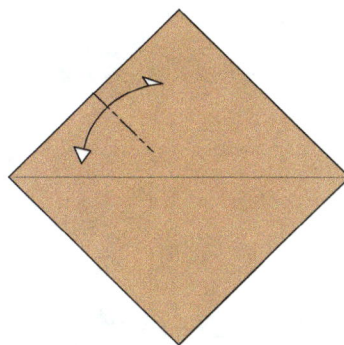

2. Pinch the top edge in half with a mountain fold.

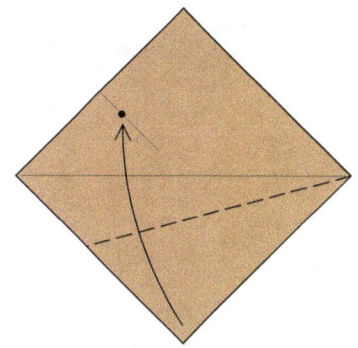

3. Valley fold the corner towards the dotted crease.

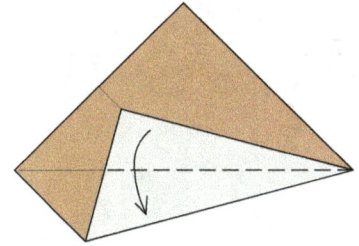

4. Valley fold down.

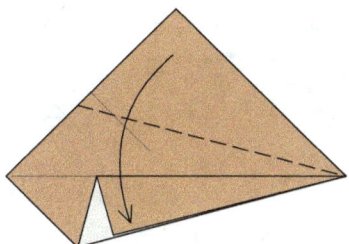

5. Valley fold down.

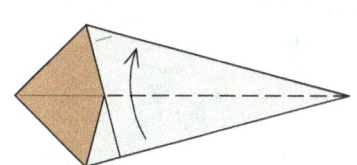

6. Valley fold up.

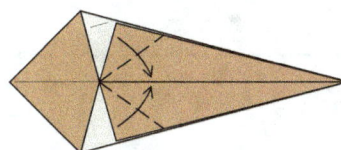

7. Valley fold the top corners to the center.

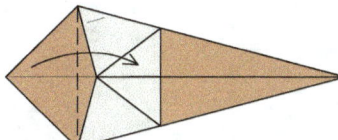

8. Valley fold the corner over.

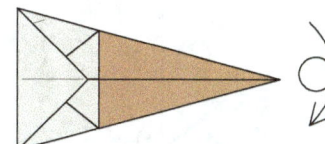

9. Turn over from top to bottom.

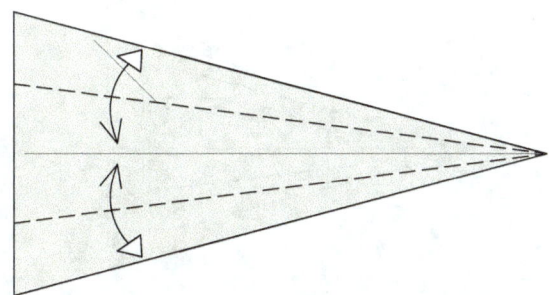

10. Precrease the top layers along the angle bisectors.

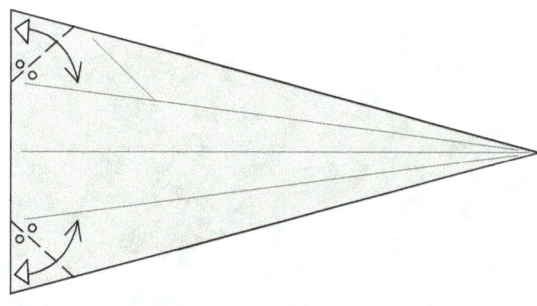

11. Precrease the corners along the dotted angle bisectors.

51

guitar

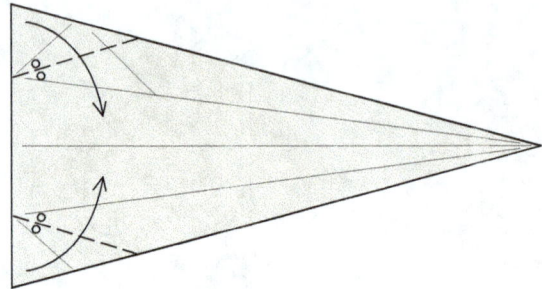

12. Valley fold along the dotted angle bisectors. The previous two creases will overlap.

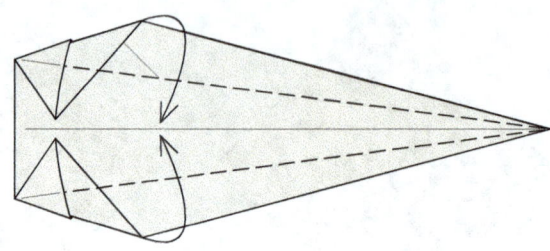

13. Valley fold the top layers along the existing angle bisectors. Part of the folds are hidden.

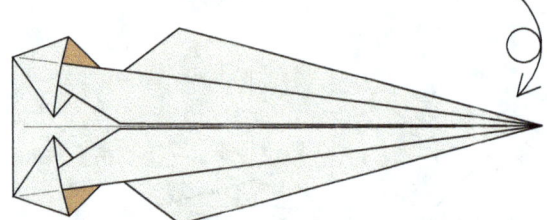

14. Turn over from top to bottom.

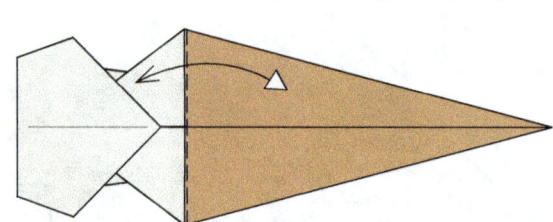

15. Precrease the flap.

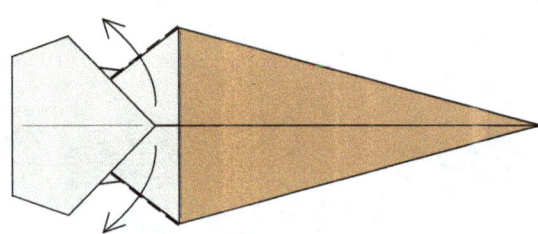

16. Open out the top flap at each side.

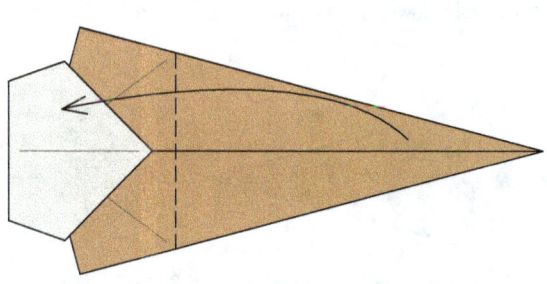

17. Valley fold along the existing crease.

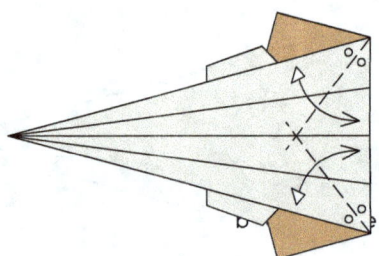

18. Precrease along the dotted angle bisectors.

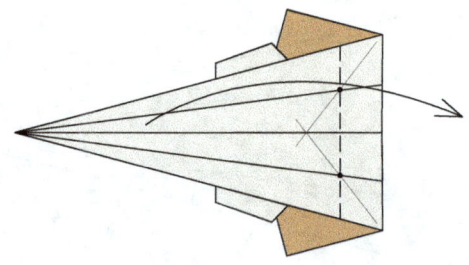

19. Valley fold though the dotted intersections.

guitar

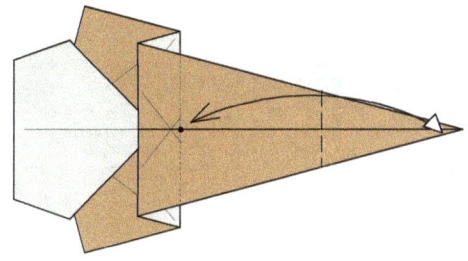

20. Precrease towards the hidden edge.

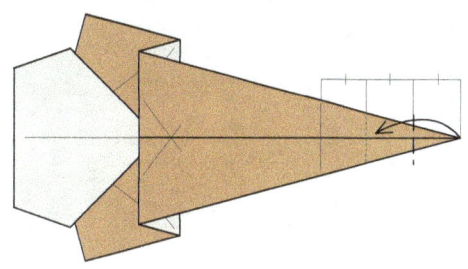

21. Valley fold along the indicated 1/3rd division.

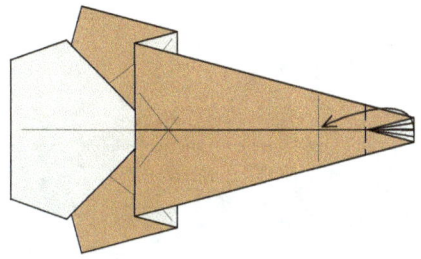

22. Valley fold towards the existing crease.

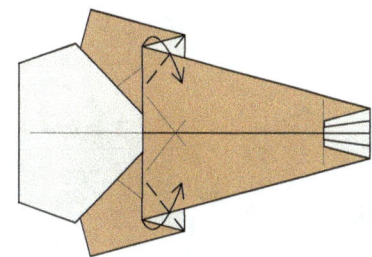

23. Valley fold along the angle bisectors.

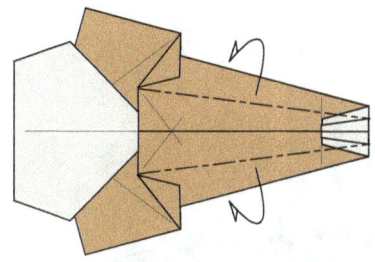

24. Mountain fold the sides so they wrap around the thick layers underneath.

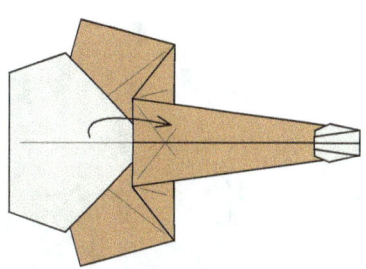

25. Pull out the trapped corner to the surface.

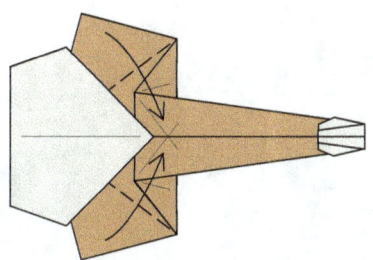

26. Valley fold the corners along the existing creases.

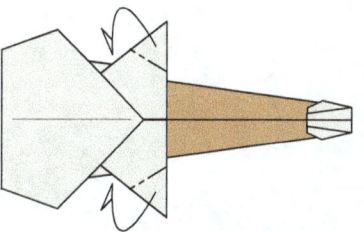

27. Mountain fold the corners, tucking their tips into the pockets behind.

53

guitar

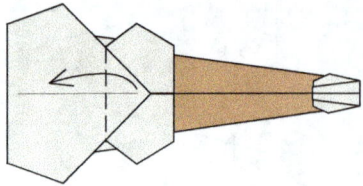

28. Valley fold the corner over from where it intersects the edges.

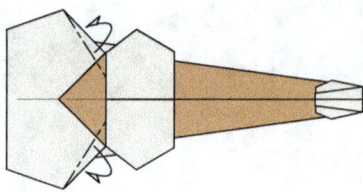

29. Mountain fold the edges inside.

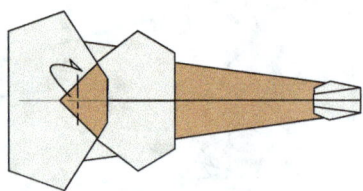

30. Mountain fold the tip in.

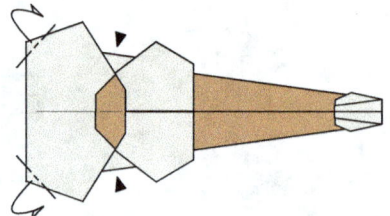

31. Round the corners with mountain folds and push in the sides by the arrows.

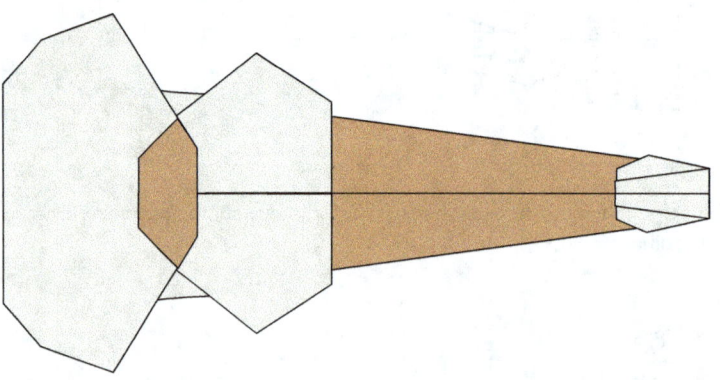

32. Completed *Guitar*.

Heart

heart

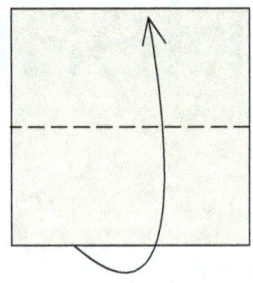

1. Valley fold the bottom edge up to the top.

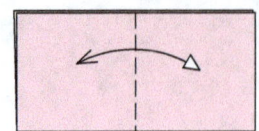

2. Precrease in half.

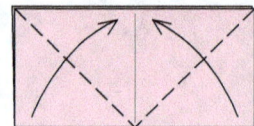

3. Valley fold to the center.

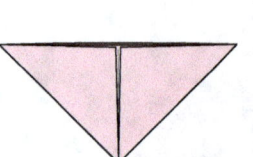

4. Turn over.

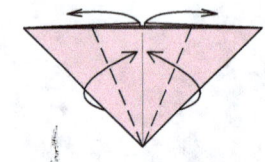

5. Valley fold the sides to the center, allowing the flaps from behind to swing forward.

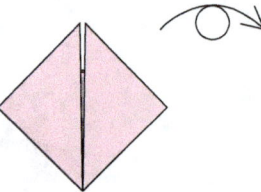

6. Turn over.

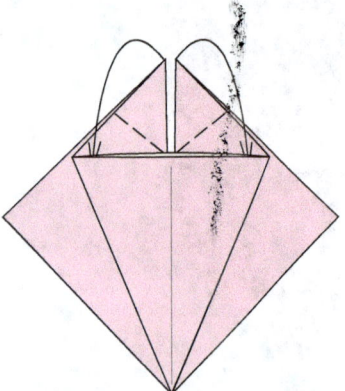

7. Valley fold the tips of the flaps into the top pocket.

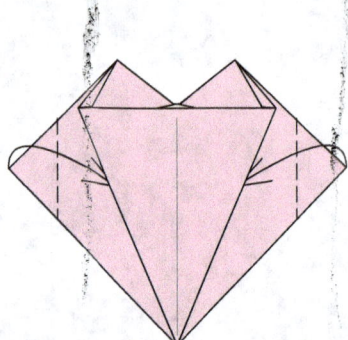

8. Valley fold the corners under the center flap.

9. Turn over.

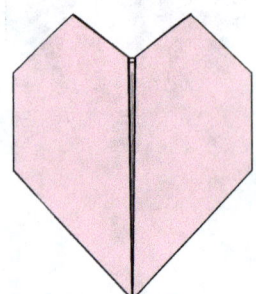

10. Completed *Heart*.

Horse

horse

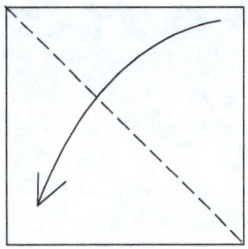

1. Valley fold along the diagonal.

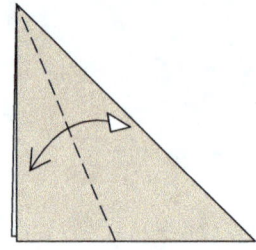

2. Precrease through all layers along the angle bisector.

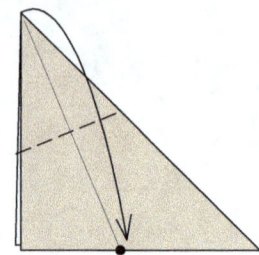

3. Lightly valley fold towards the dotted intersection.

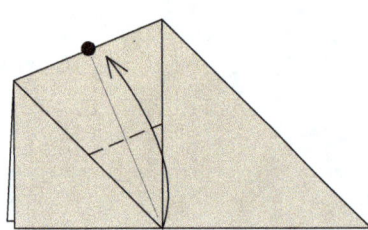

4. Lightly valley fold up to the dotted intersection.

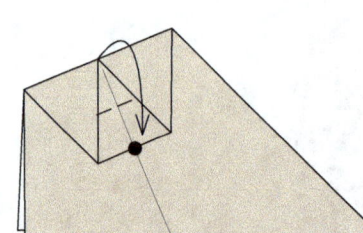

5. Valley fold down to the dotted intersection.

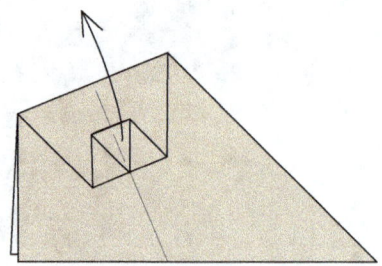

6. Unfold the pleat, leaving the last fold in.

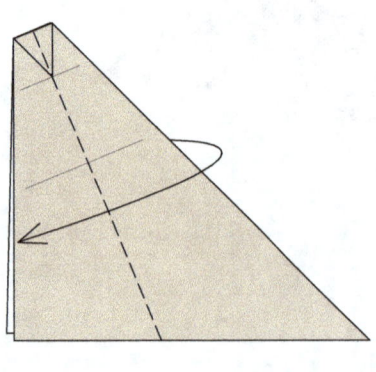

7. Valley fold along the existing crease.

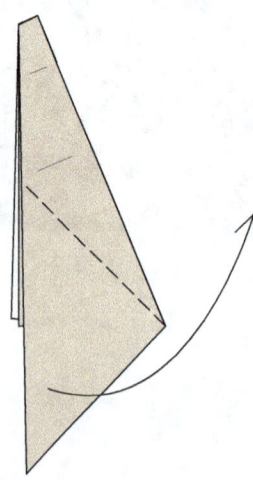

8. Valley fold up so the edge lies straight.

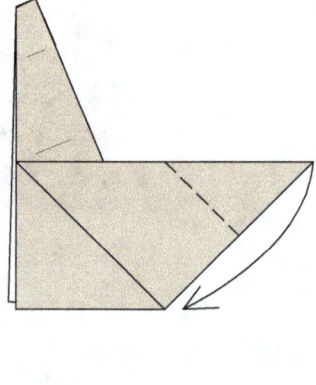

9. Valley fold the corner down.

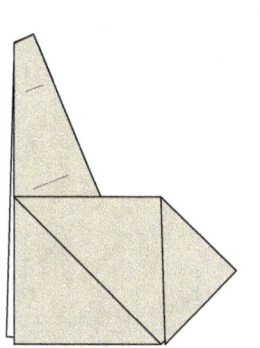

10. Turn over.

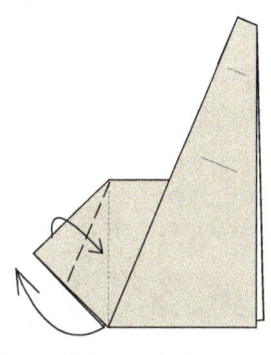

11. Valley fold towards the imaginary line allowing the flap from behind to flip forward.

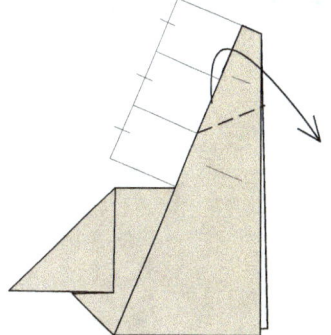

12. Valley fold down starting approximately from 1/3rd the hight of the flap.

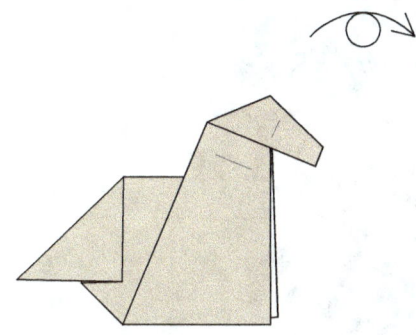

13. Turn over.

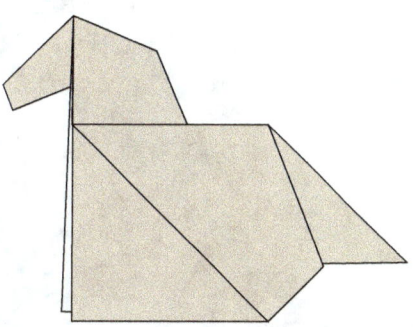

14. Completed *Horse*.

Ladybug

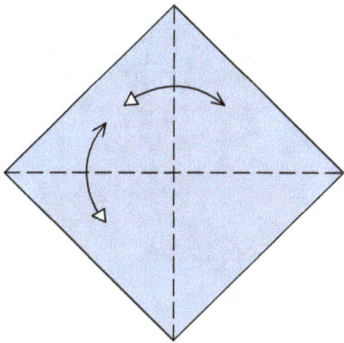

1. Precrease in half along the diagonals.

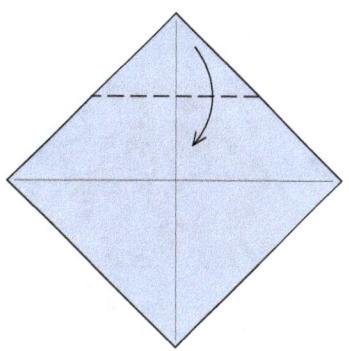

2. Valley fold the corner to the center.

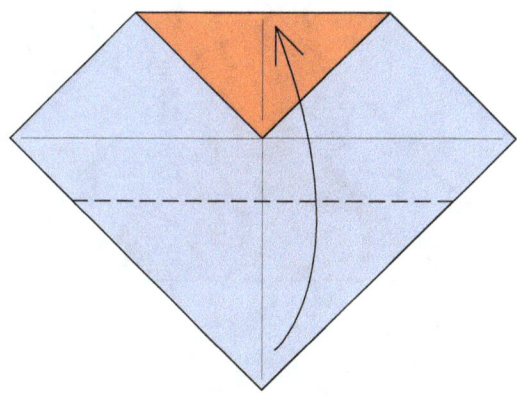

3. Valley fold to the top edge.

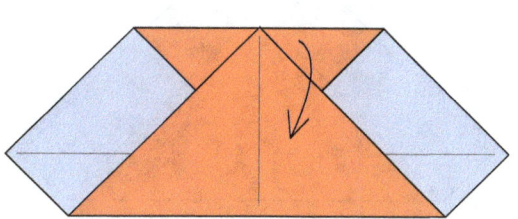

4. Pull the flap around to the surface.

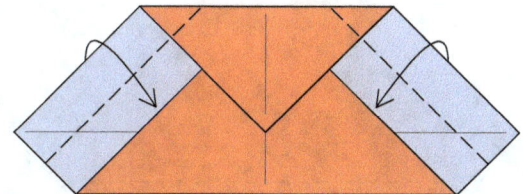

5. Valley fold the edges in.

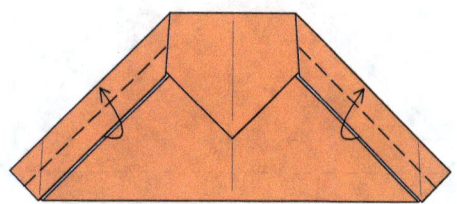

6. Valley fold the edges outwards.

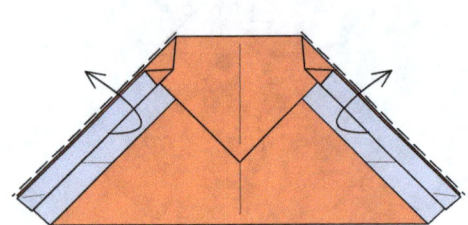

7. Swing the sides outwards, leaving the last set of folds in place.

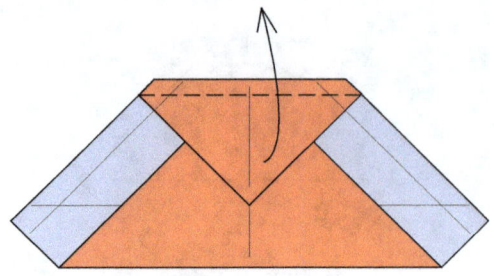

8. Valley fold the flap up.

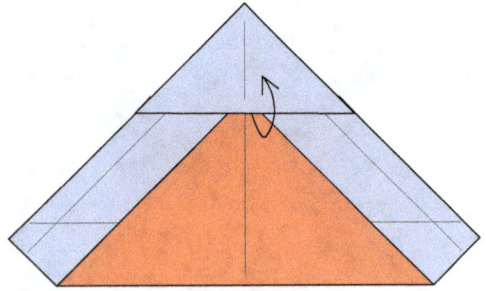

9. Pull the corner around to the surface.

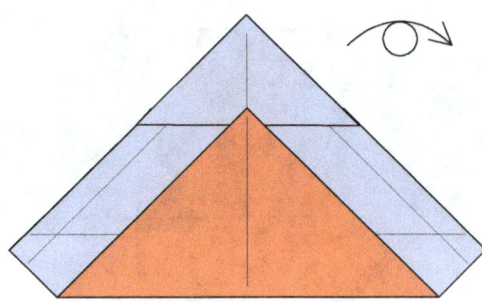

10. Turn over.

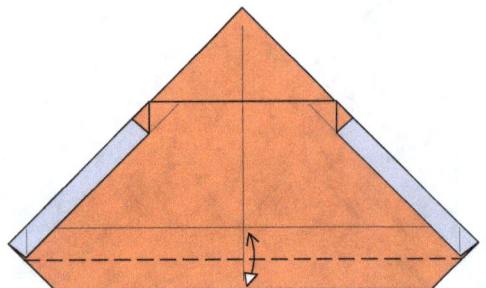

11. Valley fold to the nearest crease and unfold.

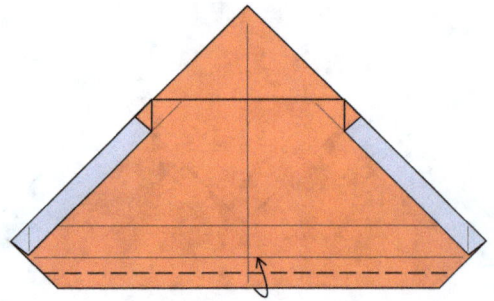

12. Valley fold to the last crease.

ladybug

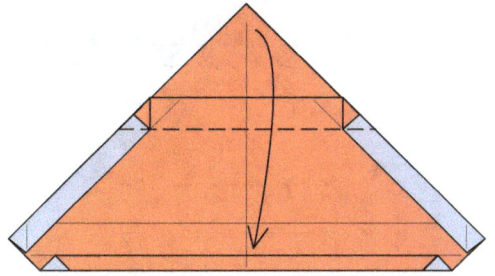

13. Valley fold the top layer down.

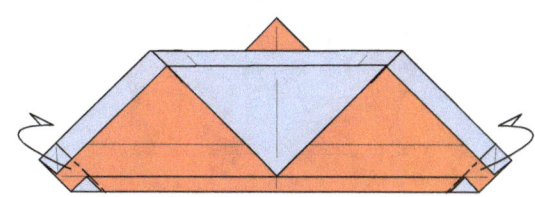

14. Mountain fold the lower edges behind.

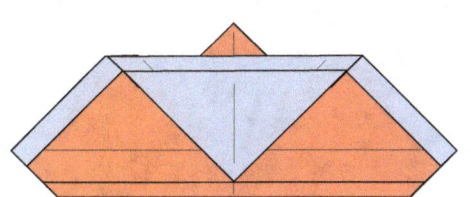

15. Turn over.

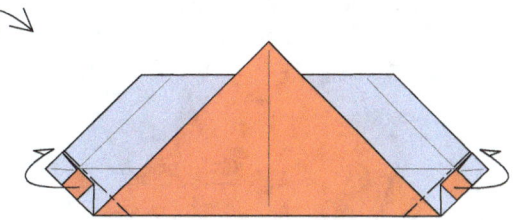

16. Mountain fold the lower edges behind.

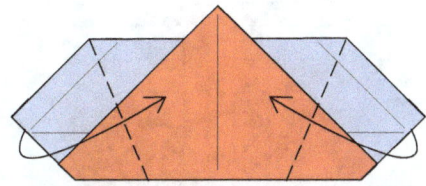

17. Valley fold the sides in, making sure the top edges align.

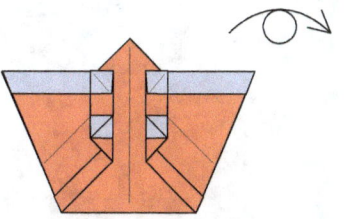

18. Turn over.

ladybug

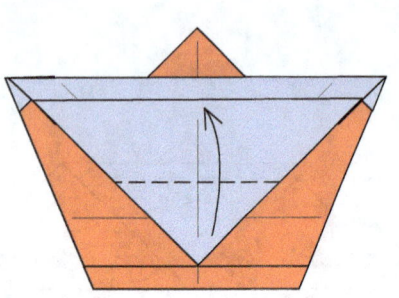

19. Valley fold the corner up.

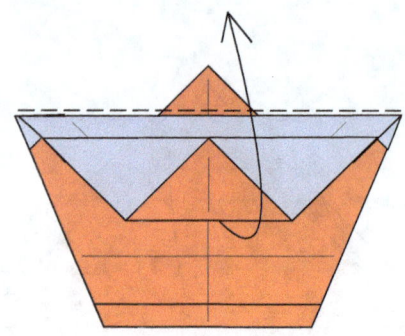

20. Swing the top section up.

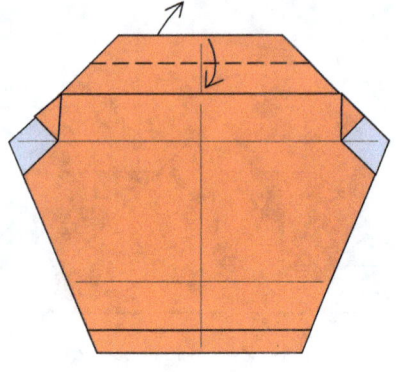

21. Valley fold down, allowing the flap from behind to swing forward.

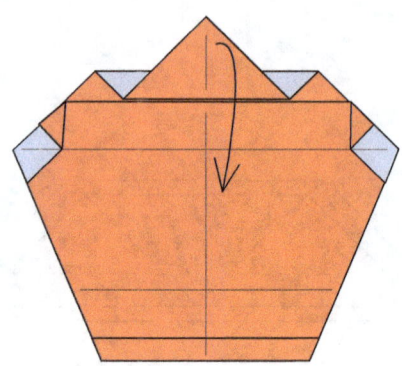

22. Swing the top flap down.

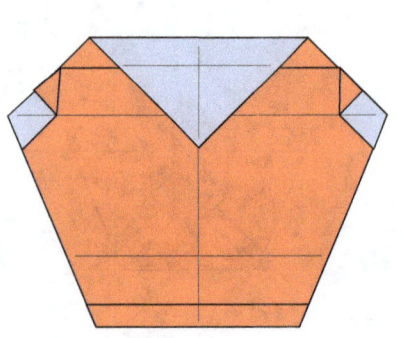

23. Turn over.

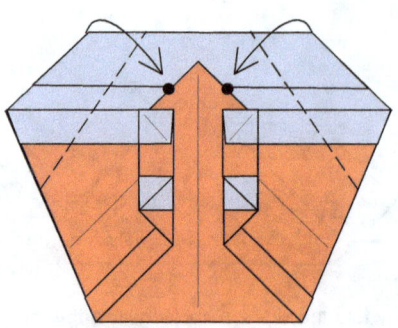

24. Valley fold the sides inwards so the corners hit the center flap.

l a d y b u g

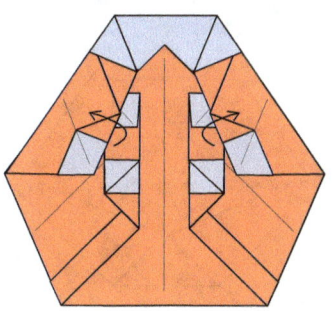

25. Pull the layers around to the surface.

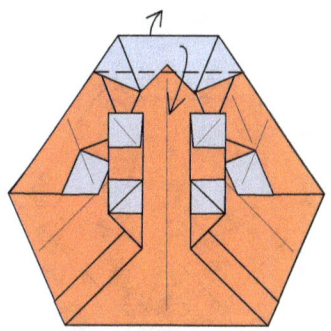

26. Valley fold the top section down, allowing the flap from behind to swing forward.

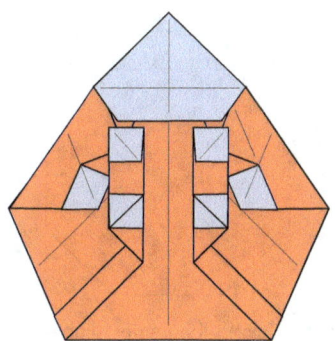

27. Turn over.

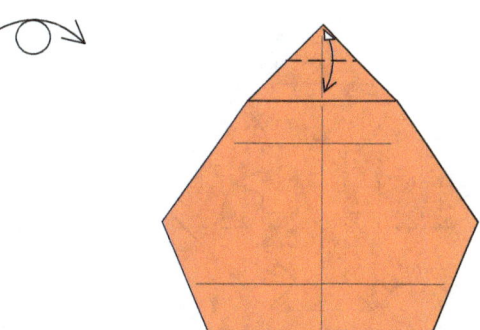

28. Precrease in half.

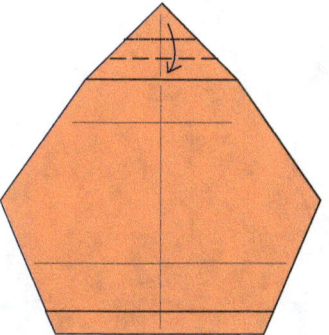

29. Pleat the flap down.

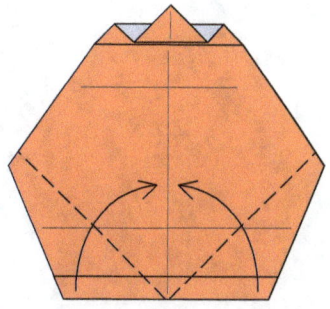

30. Valley fold the sides to the center.

65

ladybug

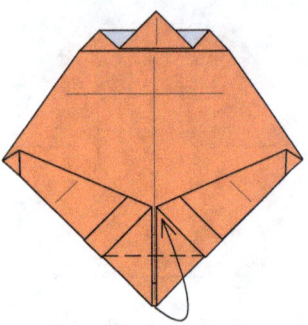

31. Valley fold the corner up.

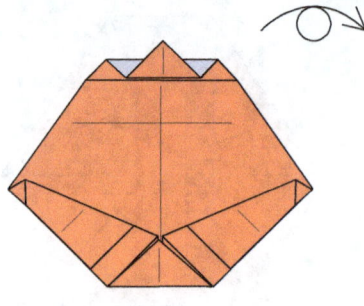

32. Turn over.

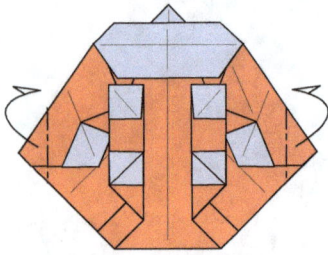

33. Mountain fold the corners behind. Do not flatten, as these corners will act as a stand..

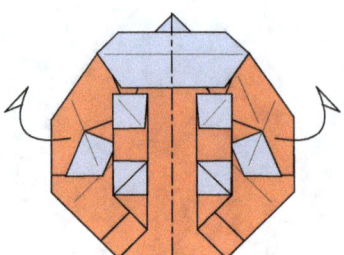

34. Mountain fold along the center slightly.

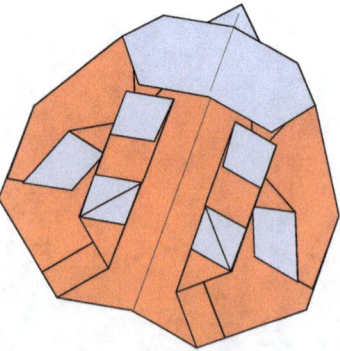

35. Completed *Ladybug*.

Owl

owl

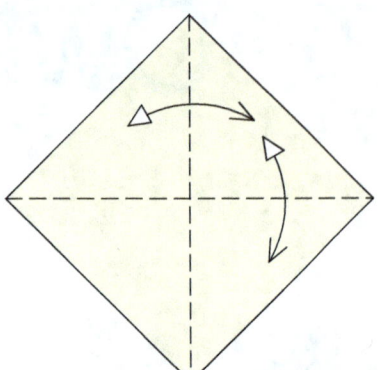

1. Precrease along the diagonals.

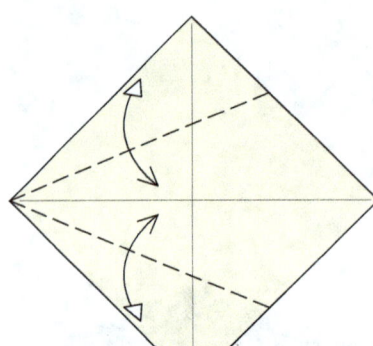

2. Precrease by folding the sides to the center.

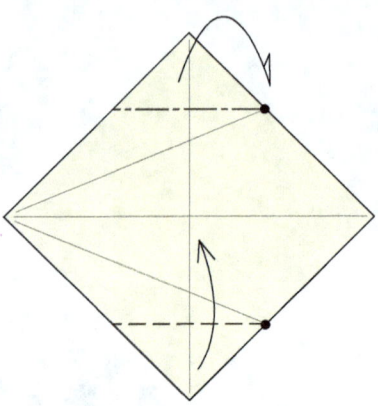

3. Mountain fold the top corner and valley fold the bottom corner, noting the dotted intersections.

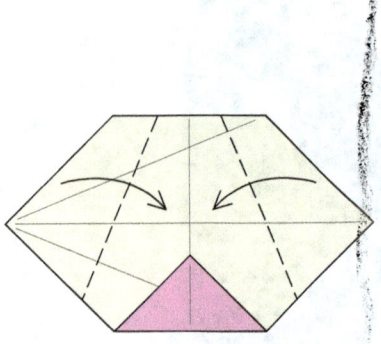

4. Valley fold the sides to the center.

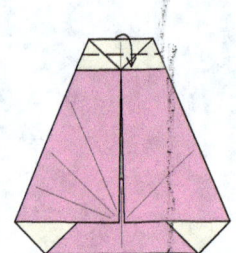

5. Valley fold the top edge down.

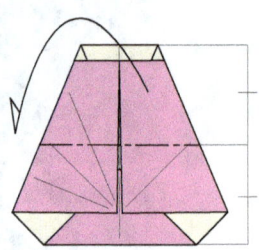

6. Mountain fold behind in half.

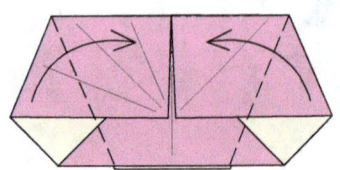

7. Valley fold the sides inwards, matching the hidden edges behind.

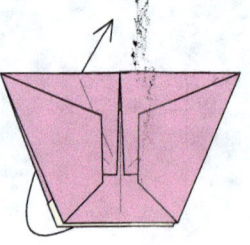

8. Unfold the flap from behind.

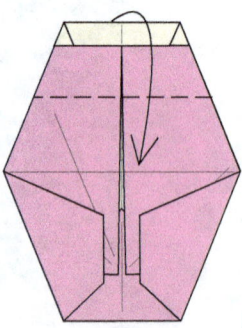

9. Valley fold towards the center crease.

owl

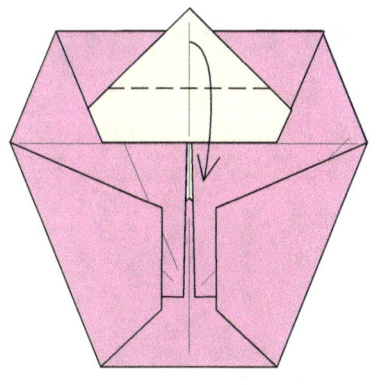

10. Valley fold the corner a little bit past the edge.

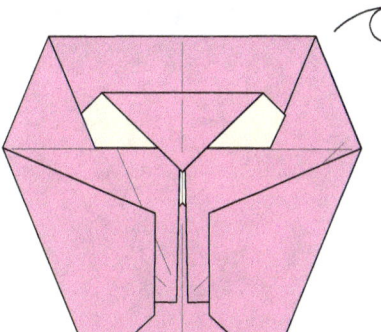

11. Turn over.

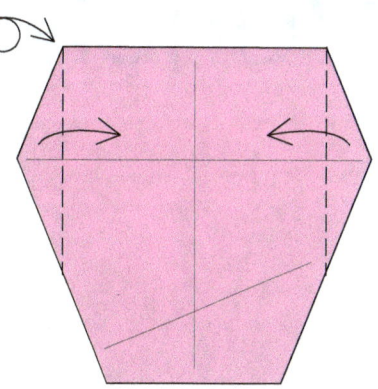

12. Valley fold the sides inwards.

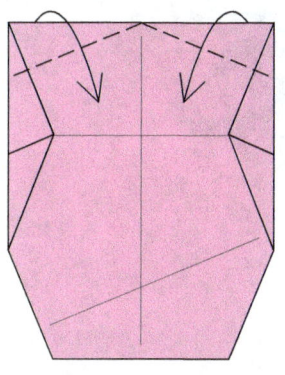

13. Valley fold the corners down.

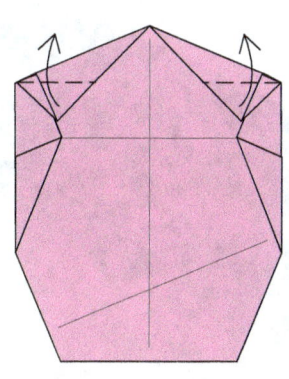

14. Valley fold the corners up.

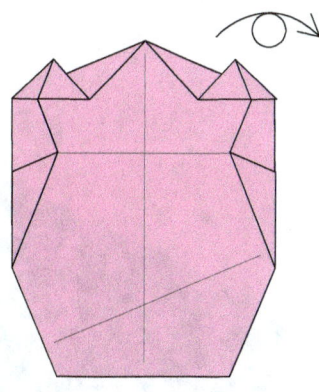

15. Turn over.

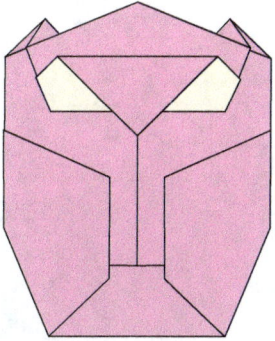

16. Completed *Owl*.

Pencil

pencil

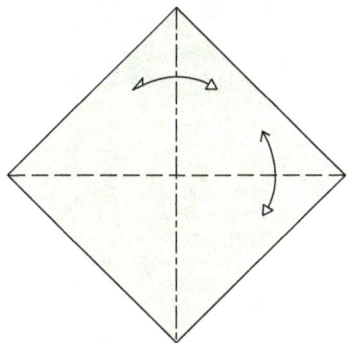

1. Precrease the diagonals with valley folds and mountain folds.

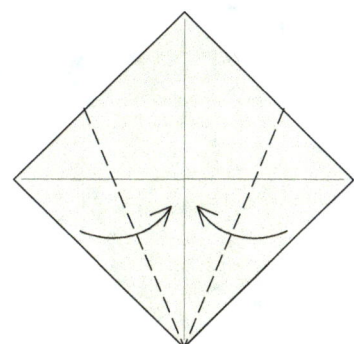

2. Valley fold the sides to the center.

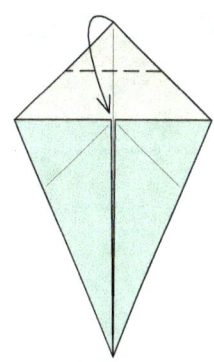

3. Valley fold the corner down.

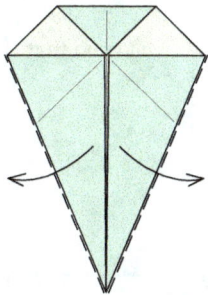

4. Open out the sides.

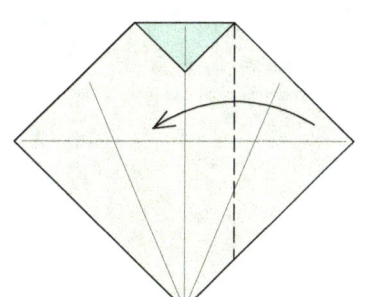

5. Valley fold the side over.

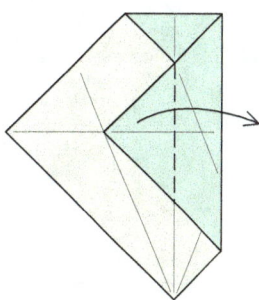

6. Valley fold over, aligning with the center crease below.

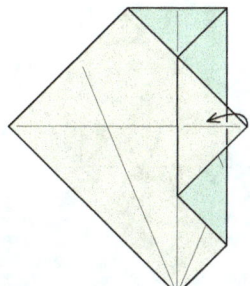

7. Valley fold the corner over.

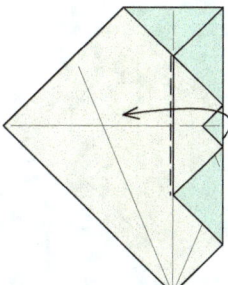

8. Swing the flap over.

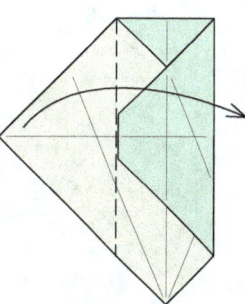

9. Valley fold the opposite side over.

71

pencil

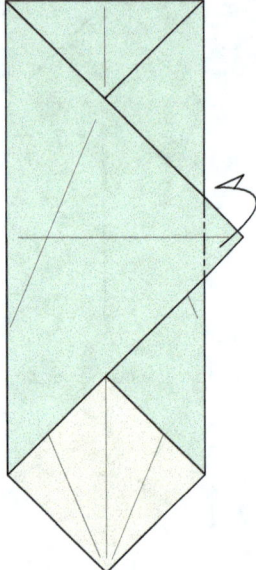

10. Mountain fold the corner inside.

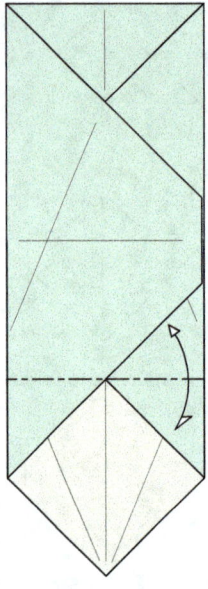

11. Precrease through the intersection of edges.

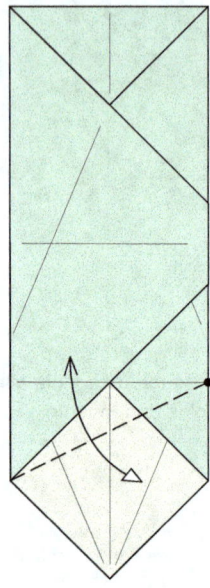

12. Precrease starting from the dotted corner.

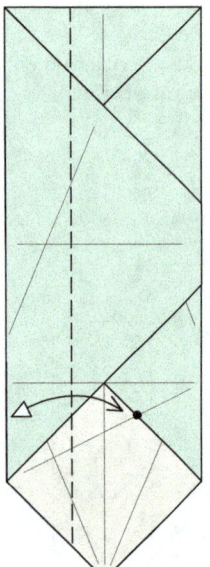

13. Precrease towards the dotted intersection.

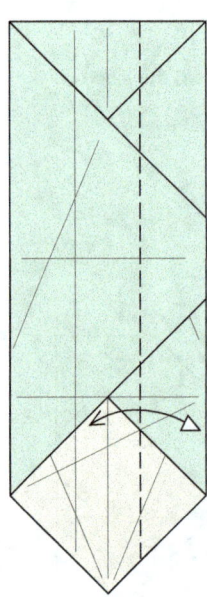

14. Precrease towards the last crease.

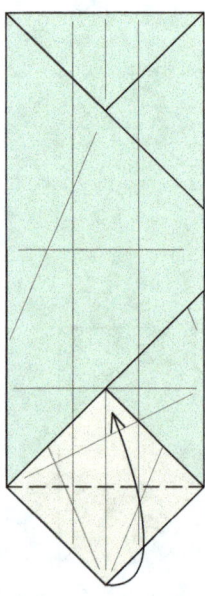

15. Valley fold the corner up.

pencil

16. Valley fold along the angle bisector.

17. Open out the top flap.

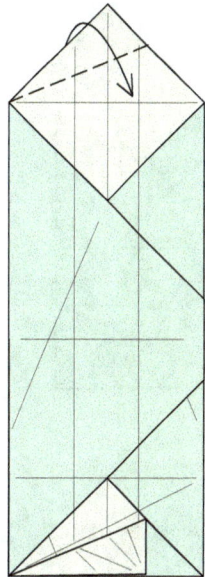

18. Valley fold along the angle bisector.

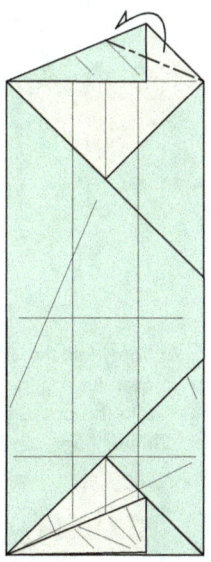

19. Mountain fold along the angle bisector.

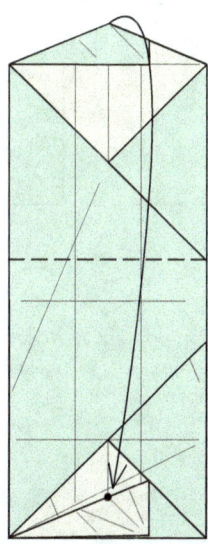

20. Valley fold towards the dotted intersection.

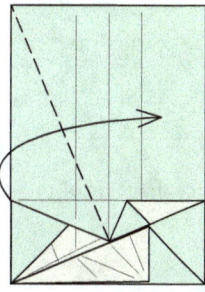

21. Valley fold the top layer over.

pencil

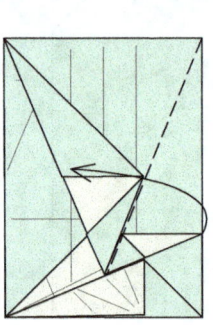 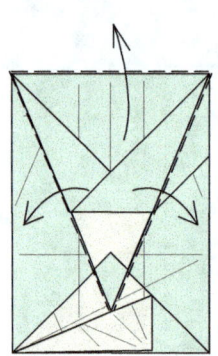  

22. Valley fold the other side over.

23. Open out the top flap.

24. Swing the top layer up.

25. Mountain fold the tiny corner.

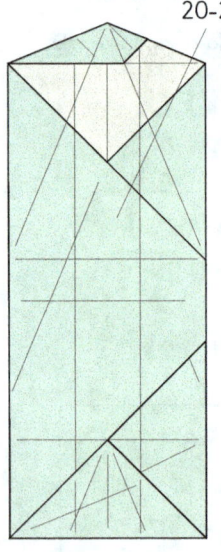 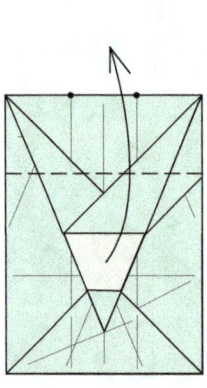 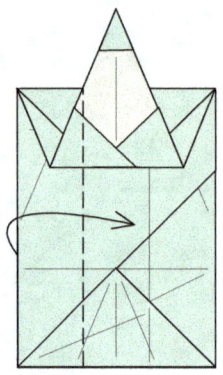 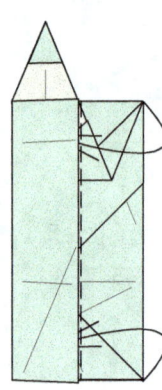

26. Replace the folds of steps 20-22.

27. Valley fold the flap up, so the edges hit the dotted intersections.

28. Valley fold along the existing crease.

29. Valley fold the other side over, tucking the corners into the pockets of the other flap.

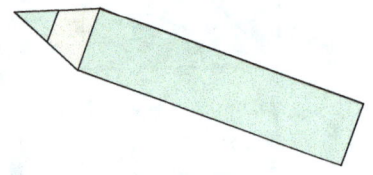

30. Completed *Pencil*.

Plane

plane

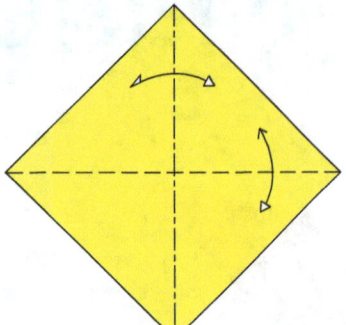

1. Precrease along the diagonals with mountain and valley folds.

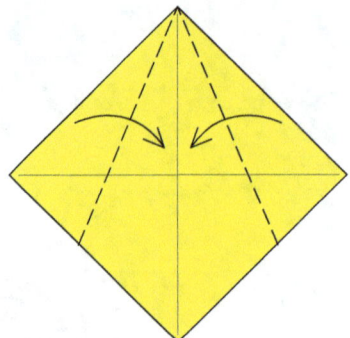

2. Valley fold the sides to the center.

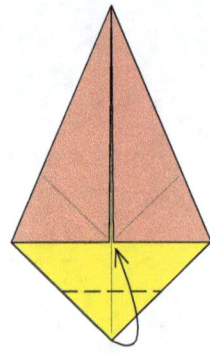

3. Valley fold the corner up.

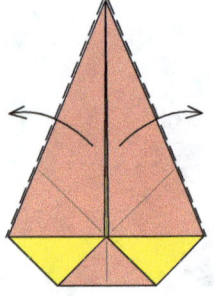

4. Open out the sides.

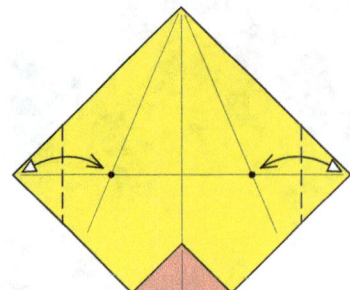

5. Precrease towards the dotted intersections of creases.

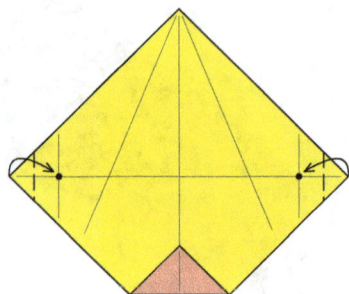

6. Valley fold towards the dotted intersections of creases.

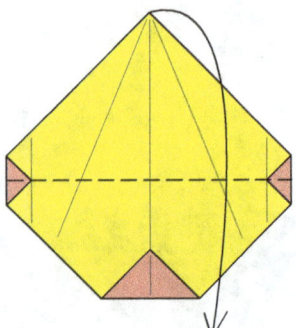

7. Valley fold along the existing crease.

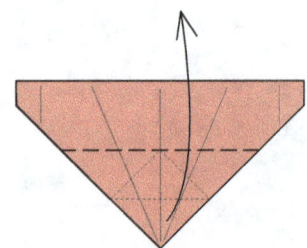

8. Valley fold up, aligning with the top of the hidden flap.

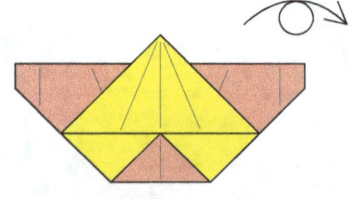

9. Turn over.

76

p l a n e

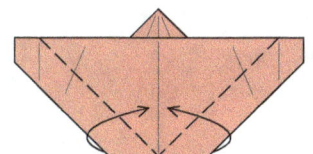

10. Valley fold to the center.

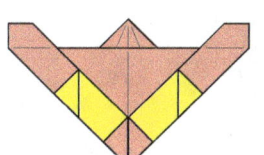

11. Turn over.

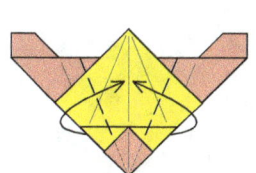

12. Valley fold to the center, allowing the folds to pass under the bottom flap.

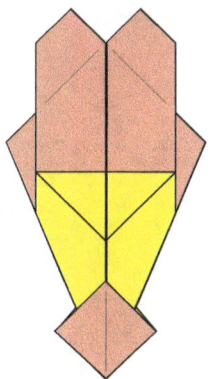

13. Turn over.

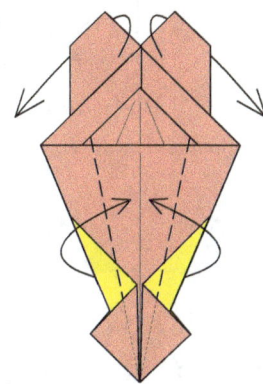

14. Valley fold the sides to the center, allowing the flaps from behind to swing forward. Parts of the folds are hidden.

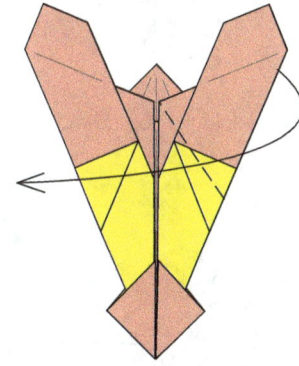

15. Valley fold the flap over so its bottom edge lies straight.

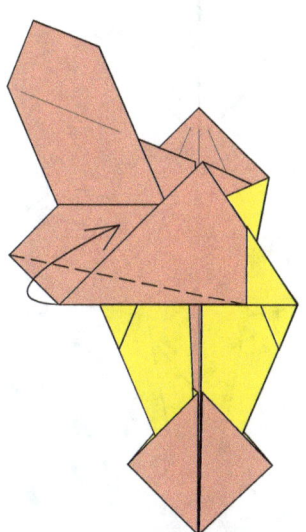

16. Valley fold the edge up.

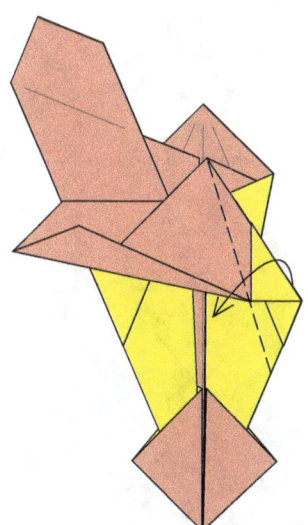

17. Valley fold to the center.

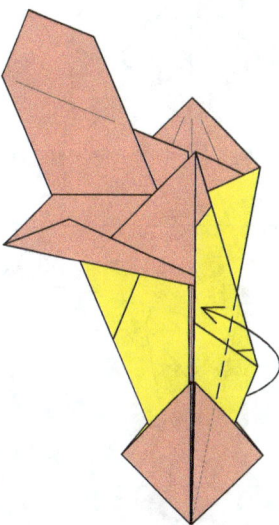

18. Valley fold to the center. Part of the fold is hidden.

77

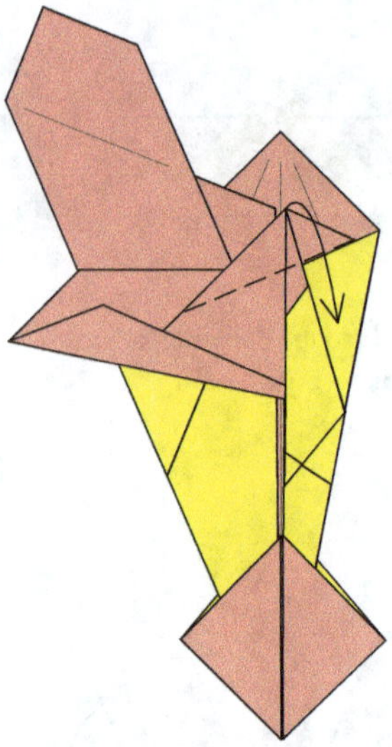

plane

19. Valley fold the flap down.

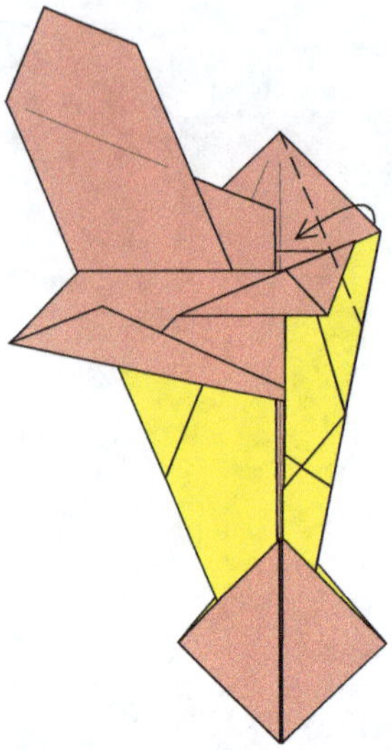

20. Valley fold to the center.

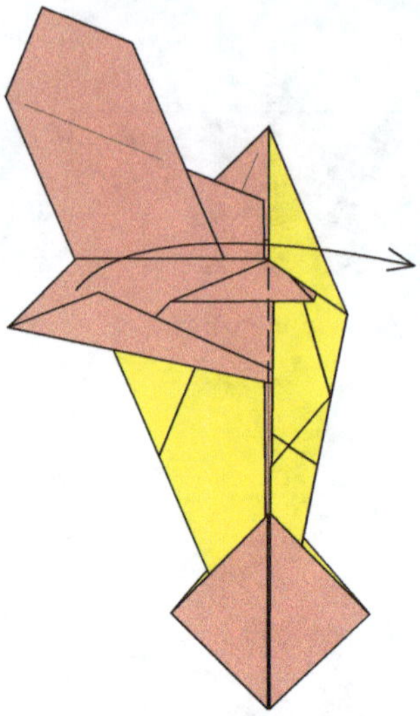

21. Valley fold the flap over.

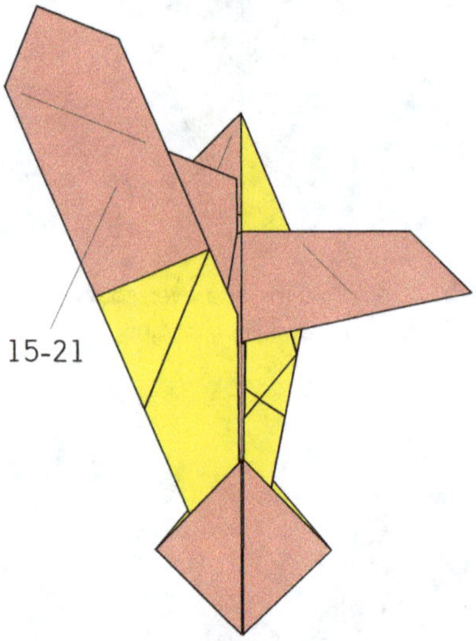

22. Repeat steps 15-21 in mirror image.

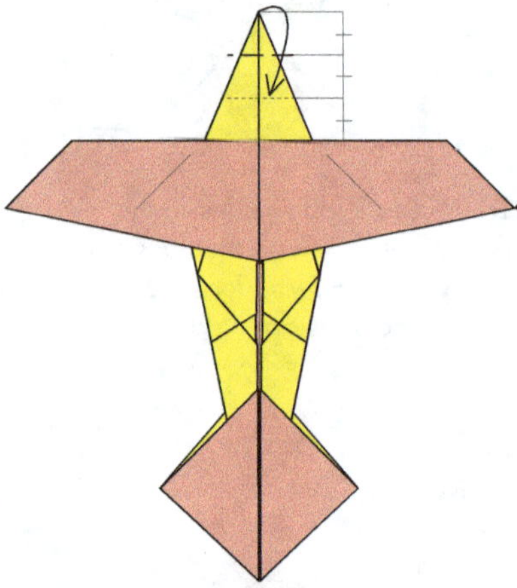

23. Valley fold the tip of the flap in.

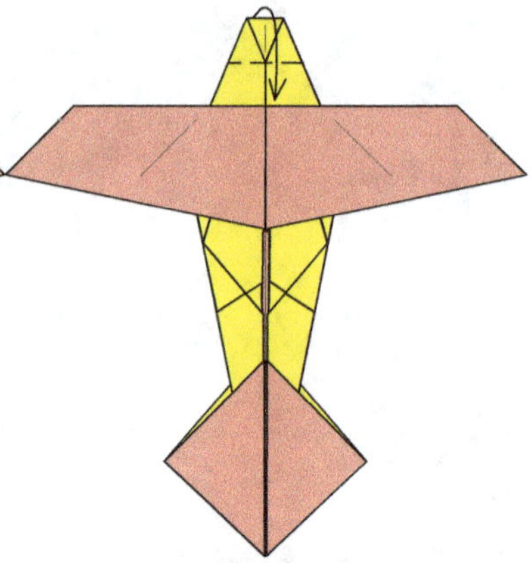

24. Valley fold down.

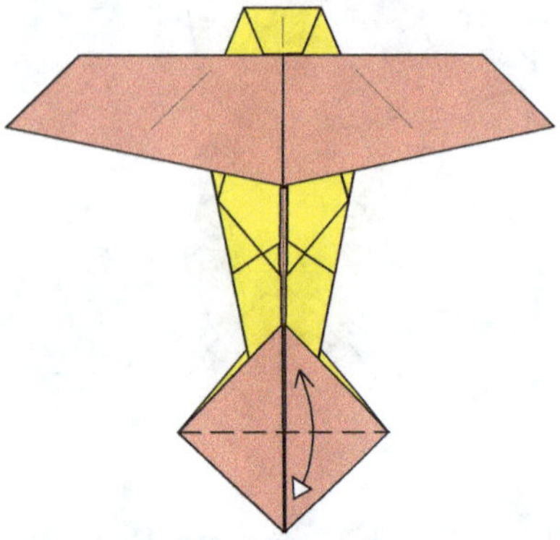

25. Precrease the top layers in half.

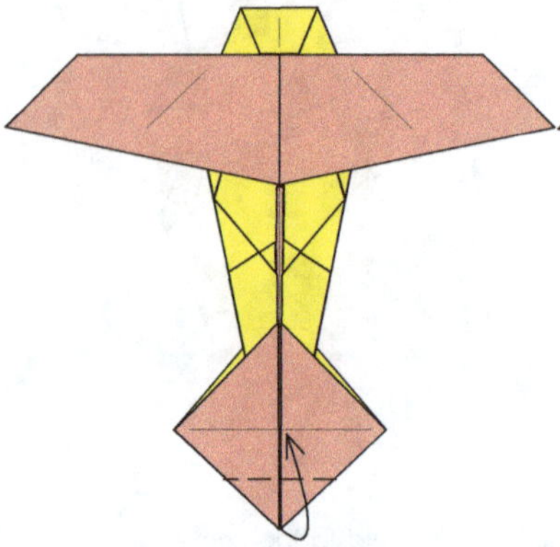

26. Valley fold to the crease.

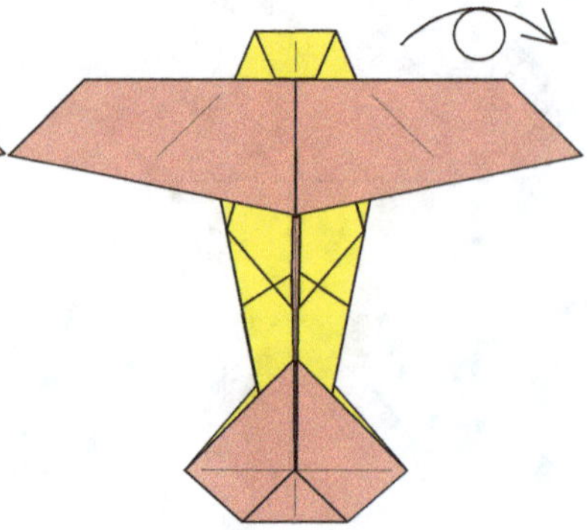

27. Turn over.

78

plane

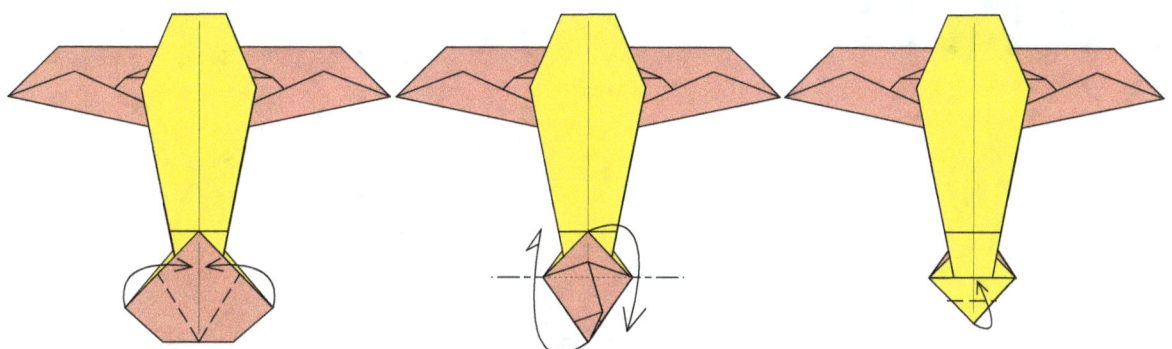

28. Valley fold the corners to the center, allowing the flaps to overlap slightly.

29. Mountain fold the flap behind allowing the top corner to flip down.

30. Valley fold to the edge.

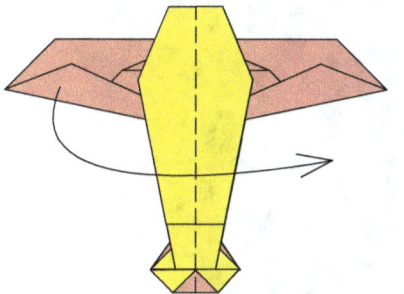

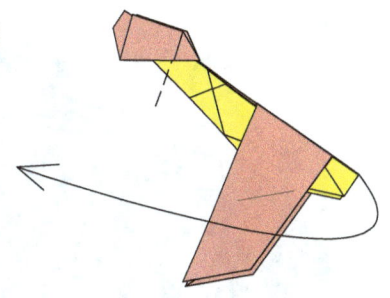

31. Valley fold in half.

32. Rotate so edge A lies straight.

33. Valley fold the bottom section over, allowing it to nestle between the cluster of tail flaps.

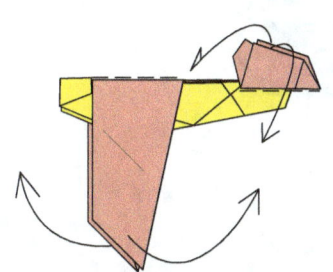

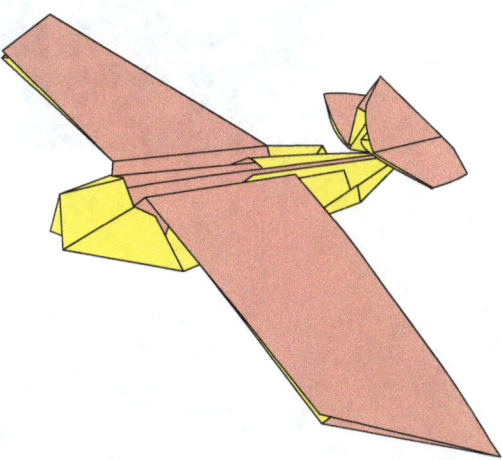

34. Open out the wings and tail.

35. Completed *Plane*.

79

Ram

ram

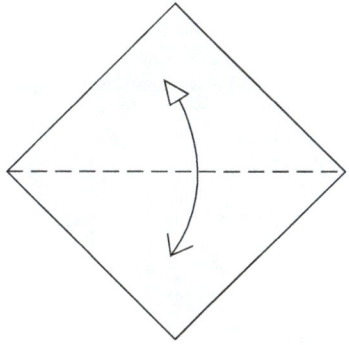 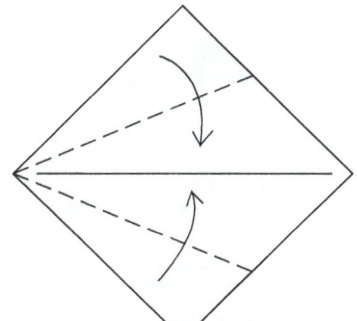 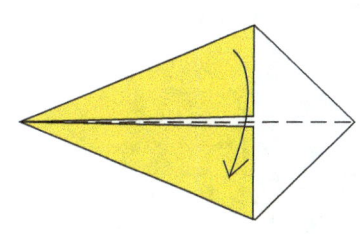

1. Precrease along the diagonal.

2. Valley fold the sides to the center.

3. Valley fold in half.

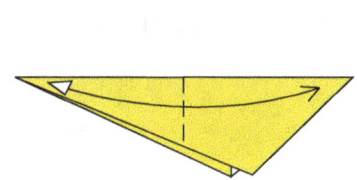 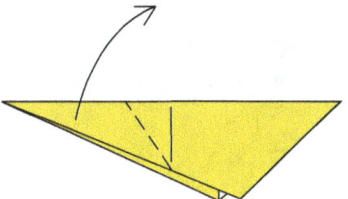 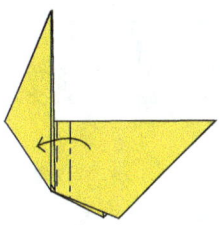

4. Precrease in half.

5. Valley fold up to the last crease.

6. Pleat the flap over. There are no reference points for this fold.

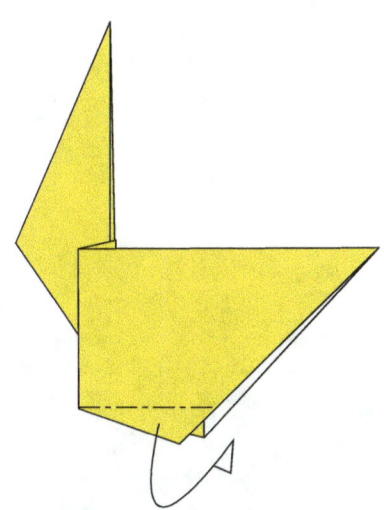 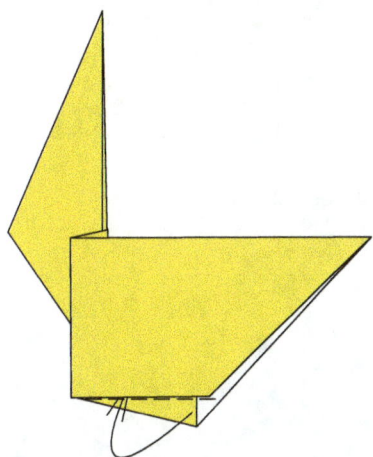 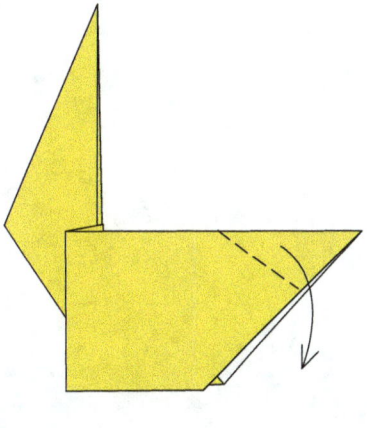

7. Mountain fold the edge inside so it lies straight.

8. Valley fold the rear edge inside to match the front.

9. Valley fold down to create a tail. There are no reference points for this fold.

81

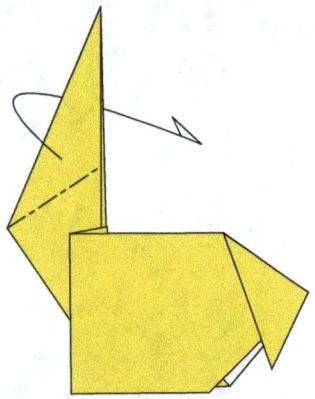

10. Mountain fold so the flap lies along the top of the body.

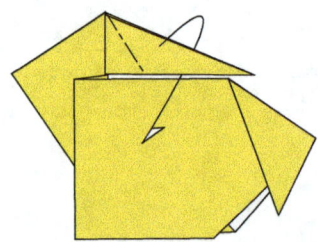

11. Mountain fold the flap, passing its tip through to lie on the surface.

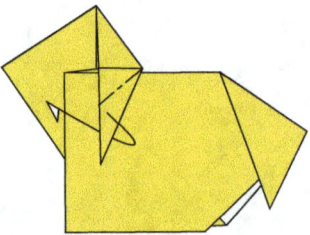

12. Mountain fold the flap again.

13. Completed *Ram*.

Sailboat

sailboat

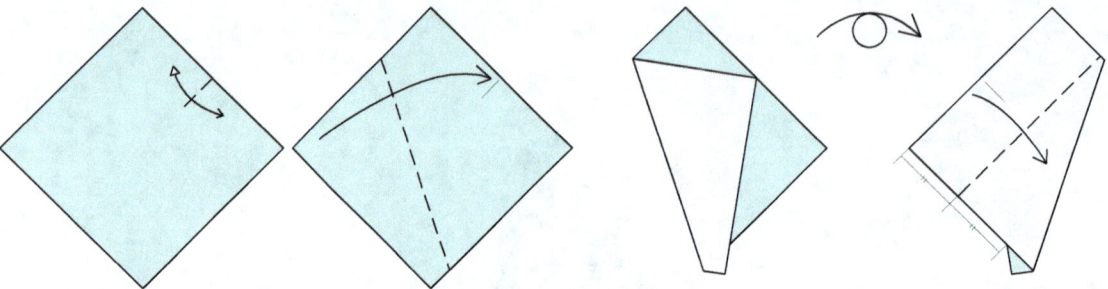

1. Pinch the top edge in half.
2. Valley fold the corner to the crease.
3. Turn over.
4. Valley fold to the intersection of edges.

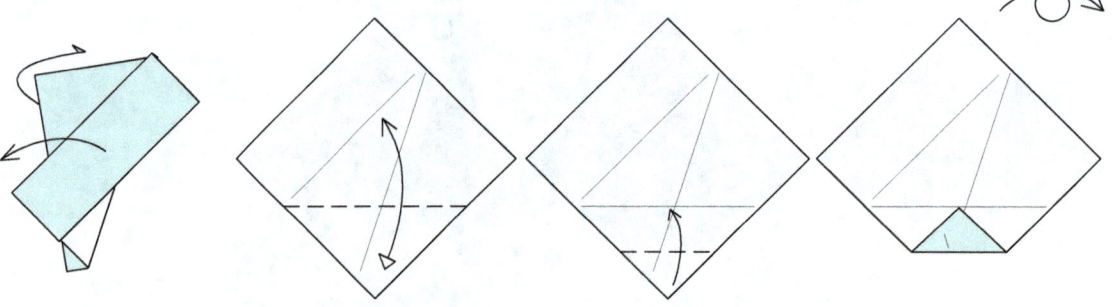

5. Open out all of the folds.
6. Valley fold up to meet the crease, and then unfold.
7. Valley fold up to meet the last crease.
8. Turn over.

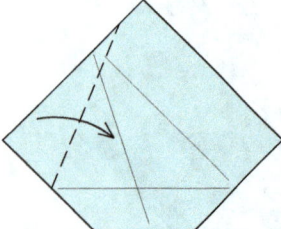
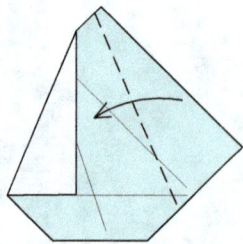
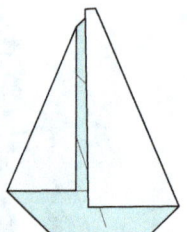

9. Valley fold over, to lie along the horizontal crease.
10. Valley fold over, so that the right edge almost meets the other sail.
11. Completed *Sailboat*.

Santa Claus

santa claus

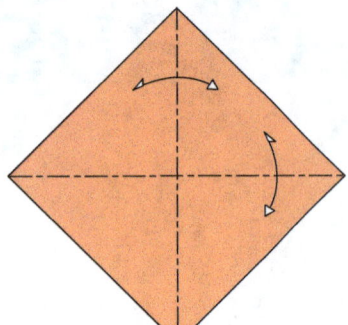

1. Precrease the diagonals with mountain folds.

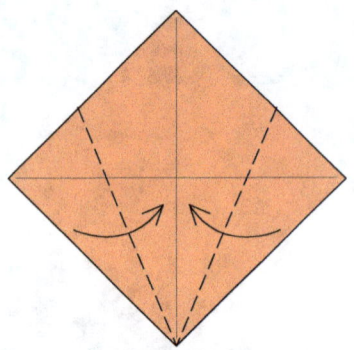

2. Valley fold the sides to the center.

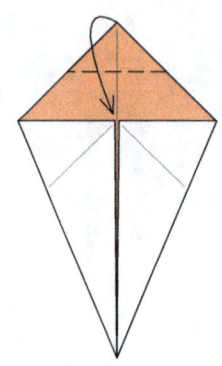

3. Valley fold the corner down.

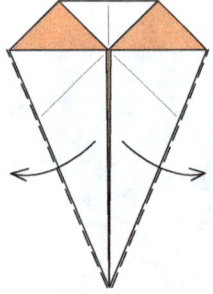

4. Open out the sides.

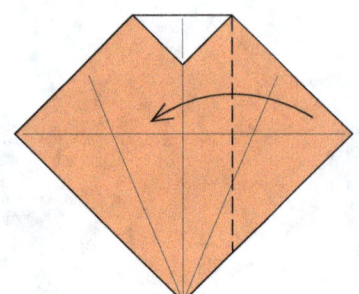

5. Valley fold the side over.

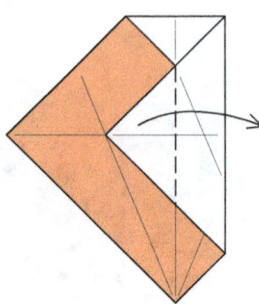

6. Valley fold over, aligning with the center crease below.

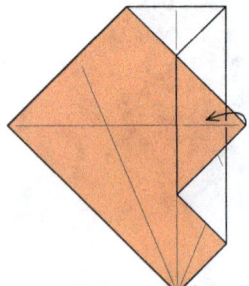

7. Valley fold the corner over.

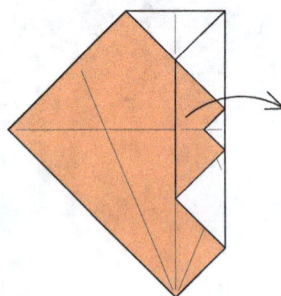

8. Open out the pleat.

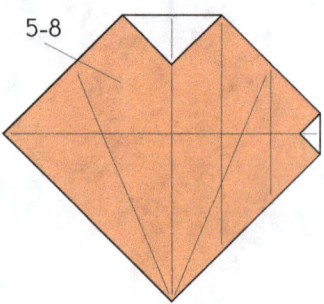

9. Repeat steps 5-8 in mirror image.

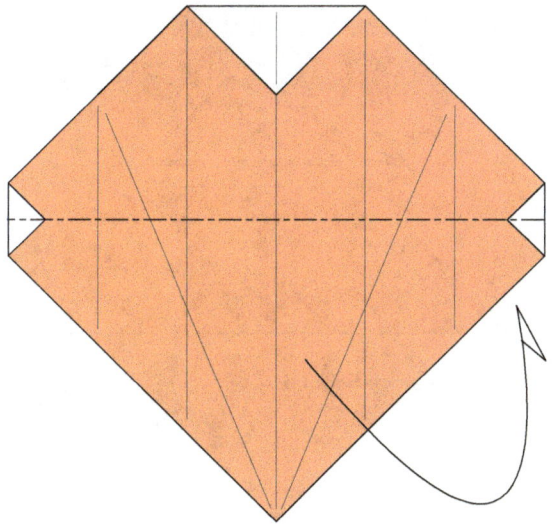

10. Mountain fold the lower section behind.

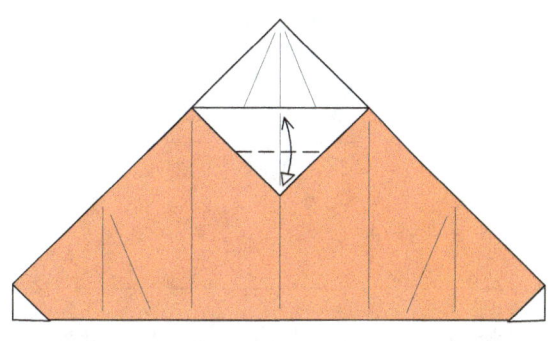

11. Precrease the top layer in half.

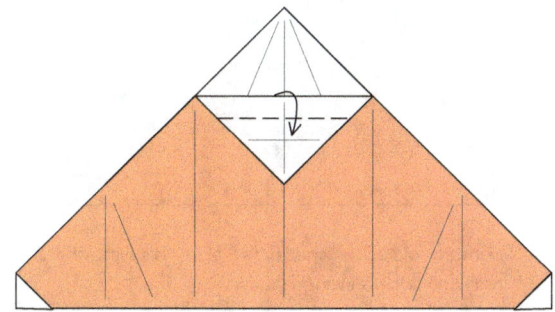

12. Valley fold to the last crease.

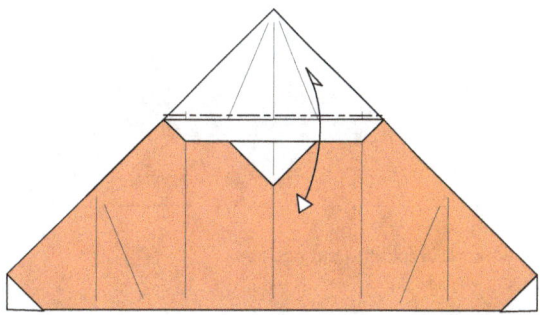

13. Precrease with a mountain fold using the folded edge as a guide.

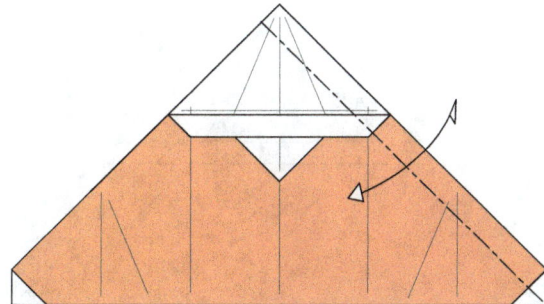

14. Starting from the bottom corner, precreases the side edge with a mountain fold.

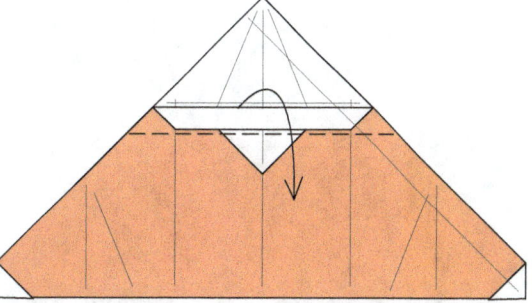

15. Lightly valley fold the top edge down.

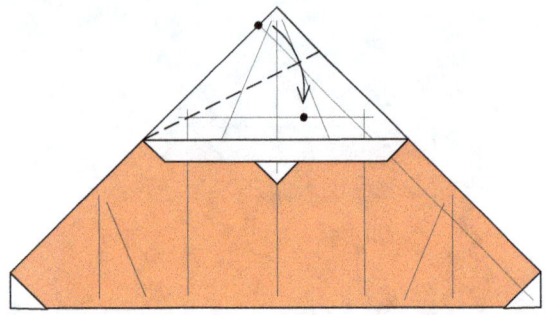

16. Valley fold so the dotted intersection hits the dotted crease.

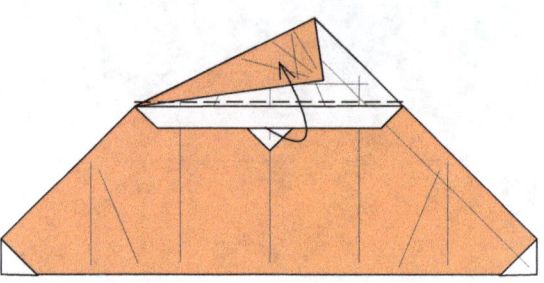

17. Swing the edge back up.

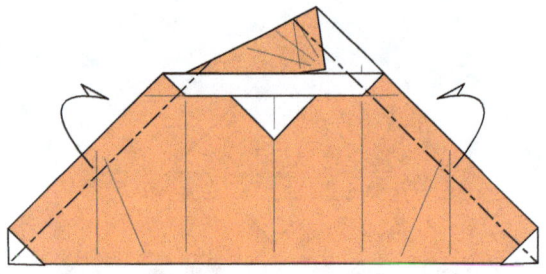

18. Mountain fold the side edges.

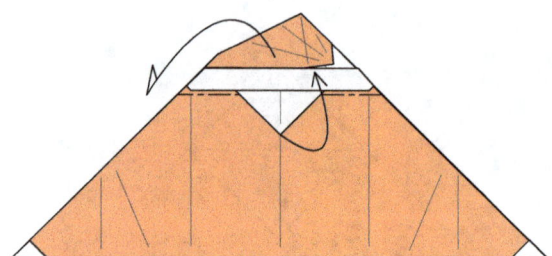

19. Mountain fold along the folded edge allowing the triangular flap to swing up.

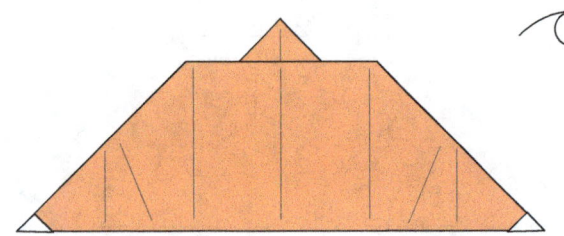

20. Turn over.

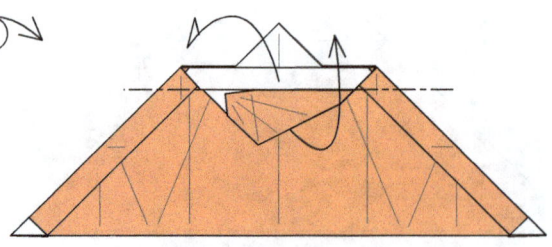

21. Mountain fold along the folded edge allowing the bottom part of the flap to swing up.

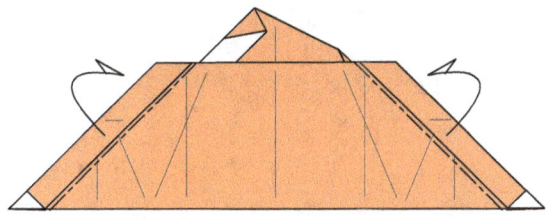
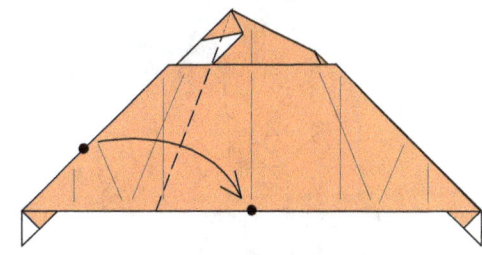

22. Mountain fold the sides.

23. Valley fold so the dotted edge hits the dotted center crease.

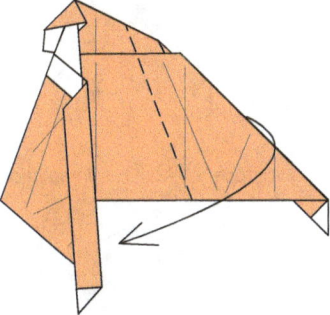
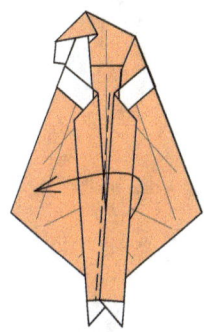

24. Valley fold the other side over at the same angle. The flaps will overlap slightly.

25. Open out the top edge.

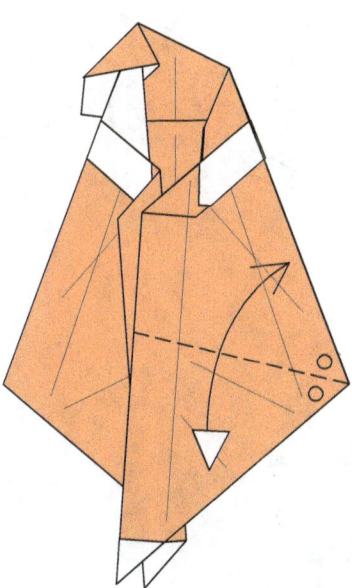
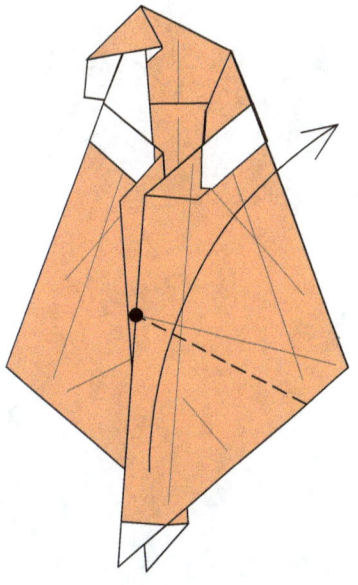

26. Precrease along the angle bisector.

27. Starting from the dotted intersection, valley fold the flap up. Look at the final step for approximate placement.

santa claus

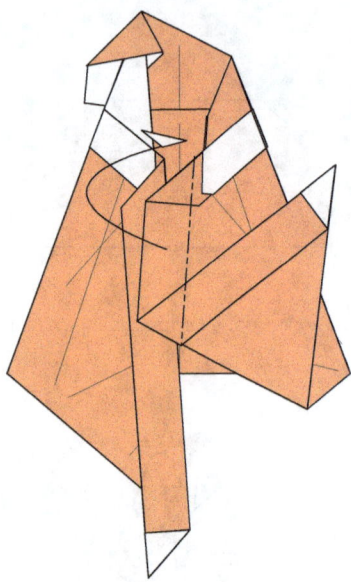

28. Mountain fold the edge inside.

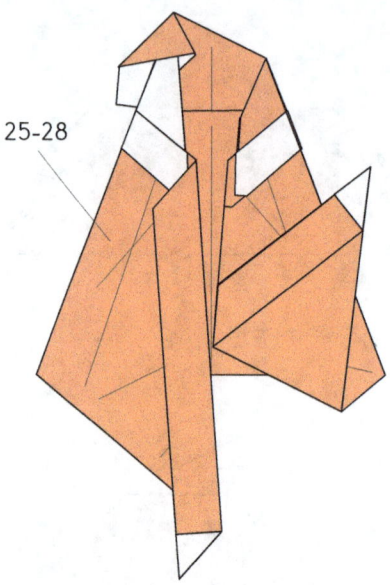

29. Repeat steps 25-28 in mirror image.

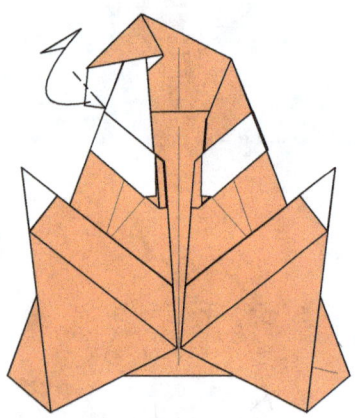

30. Mountain fold the corner.

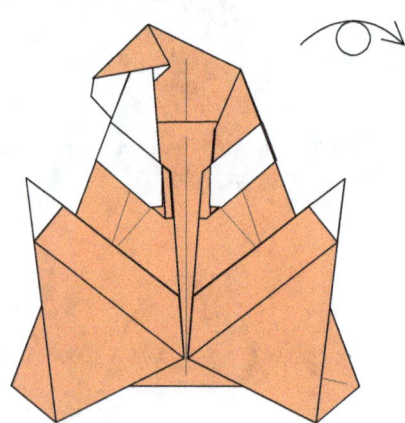

31. Turn over.

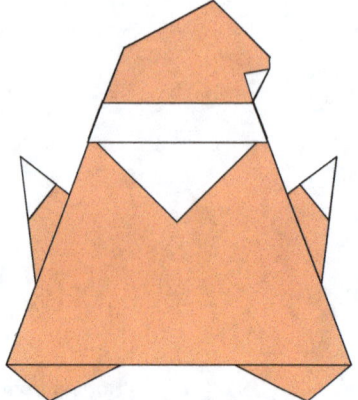

32. Completed *Santa Claus*.

Shirt

shirt

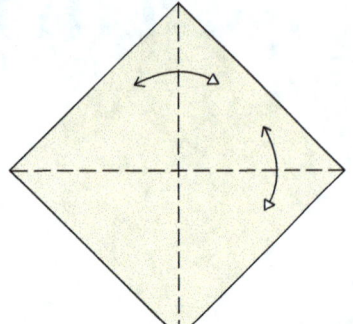

1. Precrease along the diagonals.

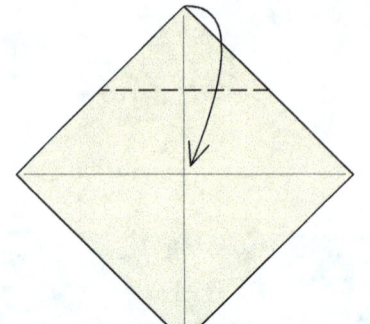

2. Valley fold to the center.

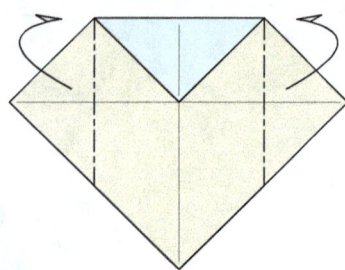

3. Mountain fold the corners behind to the center.

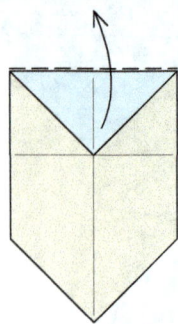

4. Open out the top flap.

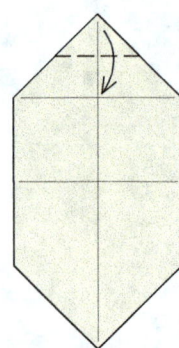

5. Valley fold to the crease.

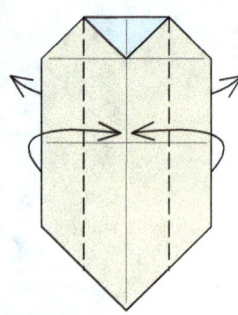

6. Valley fold the sides to the center, allowing the flaps from behind to swing forward.

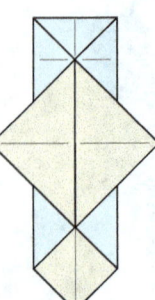

7. Turn over.

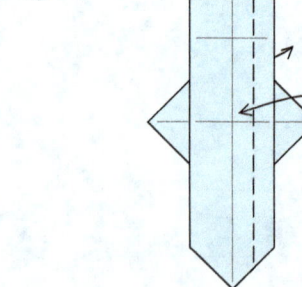

8. Valley fold the edges to the center, allowing the flaps from behind to swing forward.

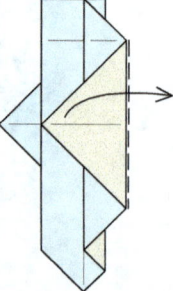

9. Open out the top flap.

— s h i r t —

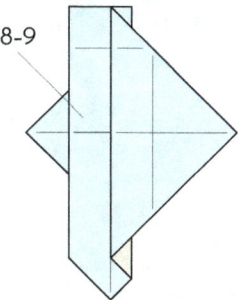
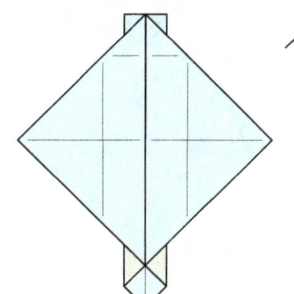
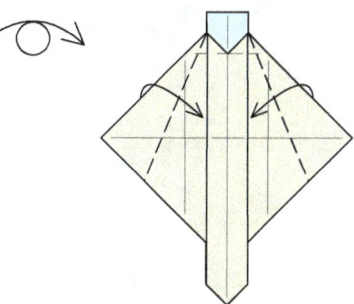

10. Repeat steps 8-9 in mirror image.

11. Turn over.

12. Valley fold the sides to the folded edges.

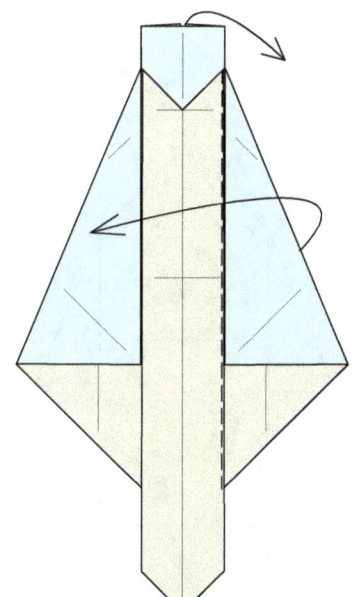
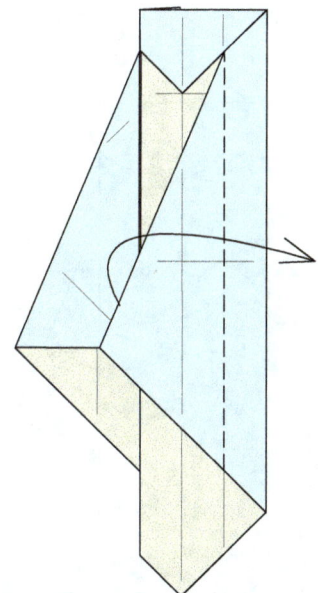
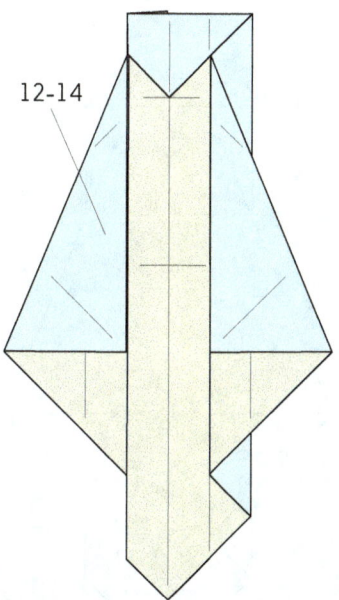

13. Swing the flap over, allowing the small flap from behind to open out.

14. Lightly valley fold the flap over.

15. Repeat steps 12-14 in mirror image.

— s h i r t —

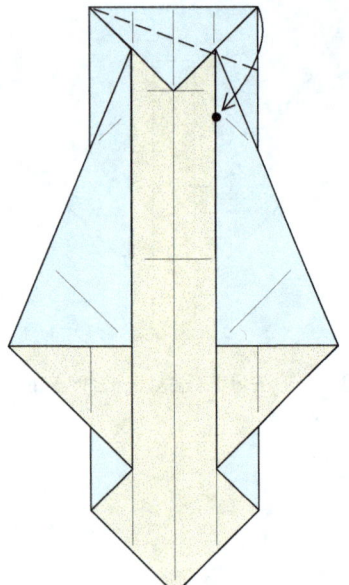 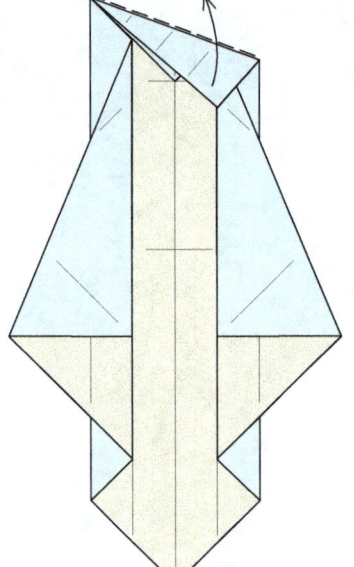 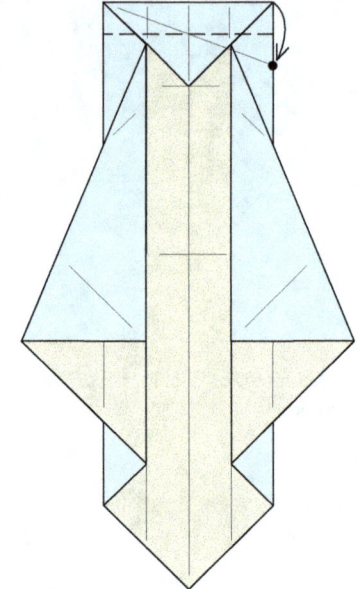

16. Valley fold the corner down so it hits the dotted edge.

17. Open the flap back up.

18. Valley fold to the dotted crease.

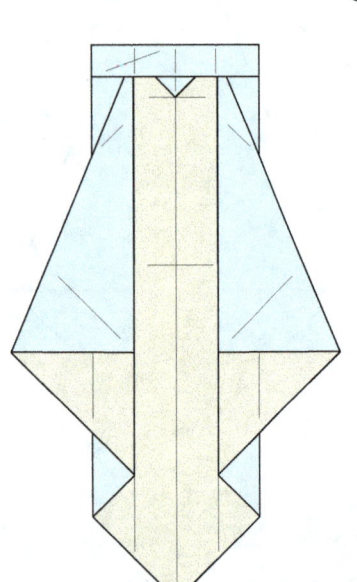 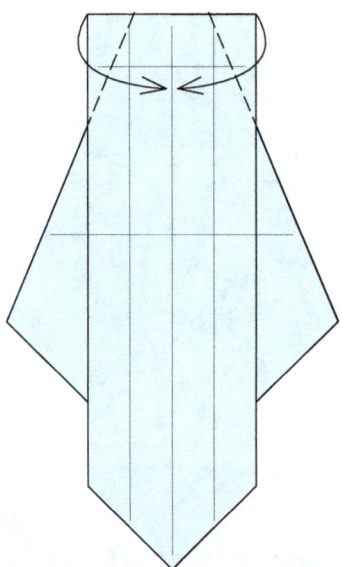 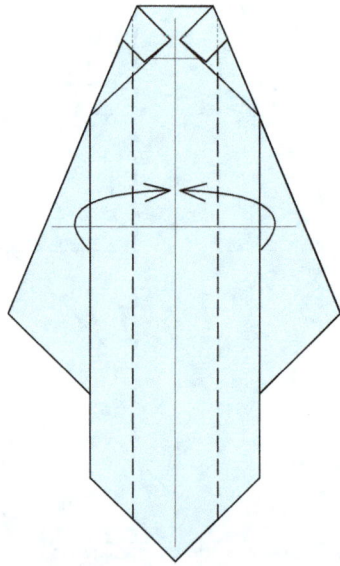

19. Turn over.

20. Valley fold the sides, aligning with the hidden edges below. The corners will *not* quite reach the center.

21. Valley fold the sides to the center. Parts of the fold are hidden.

shirt

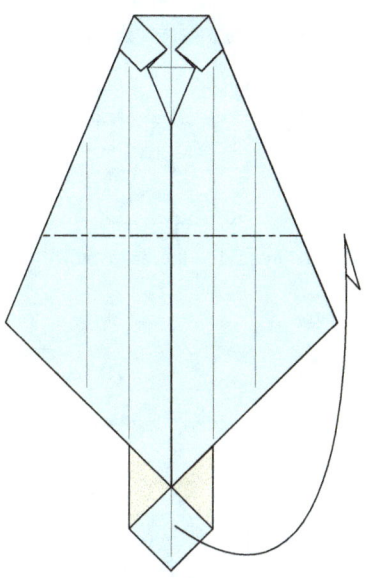
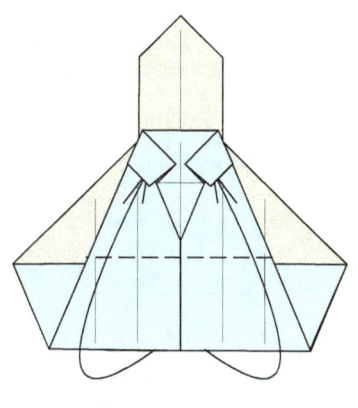
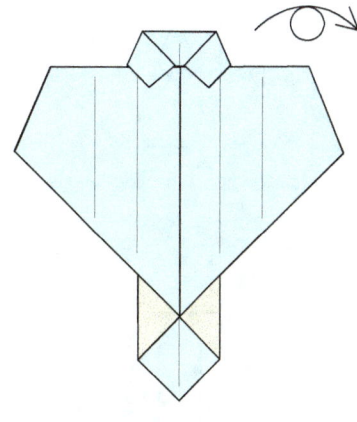

22. Mountain fold along the existing crease.

23. Valley fold the bottom edge to tuck under the top flaps, allowing the flap from behind to swing forward.

24. Turn over.

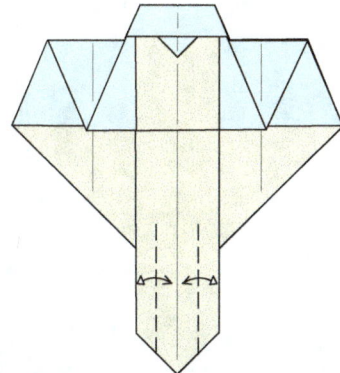
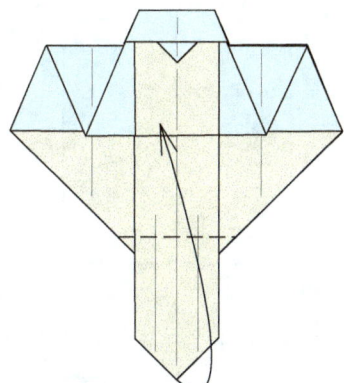
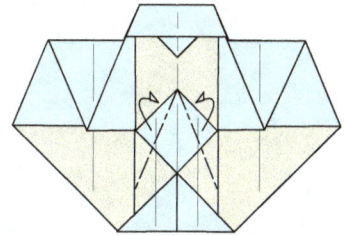

25. Precrease the sides in half.

26. Valley fold the flap up.

27. Mountain fold the sides along the angle bisectors. You can temporarily swing down the flap.

95

shirt

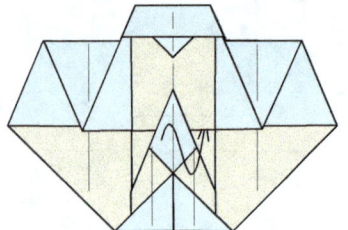

28. Tuck the tip of the flap under.

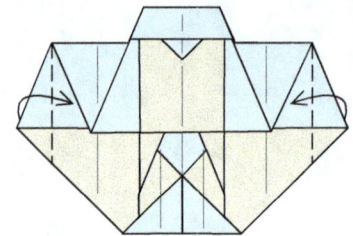

29. Valley fold the sides in.

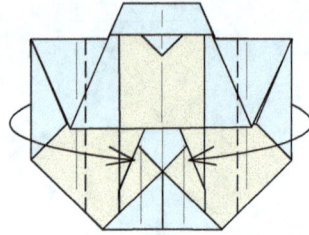

30. Valley fold to the creases.

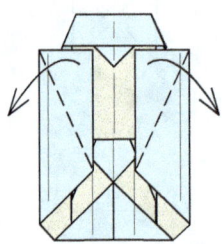

31. Valley fold the sides outwards.

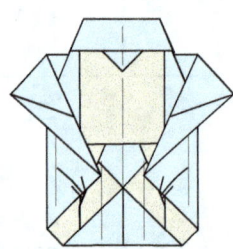

32. Tuck the corners of the flaps under the center flap.

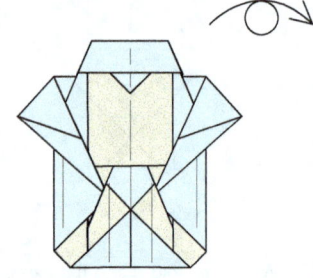

33. Turn over.

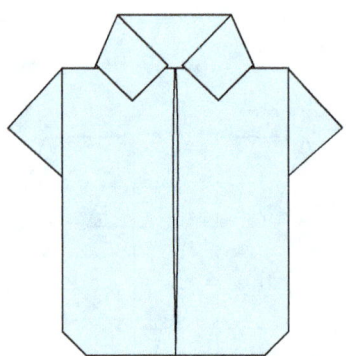

34. Completed *Shirt*.

Skunk

skunk

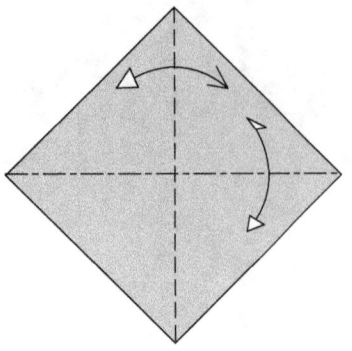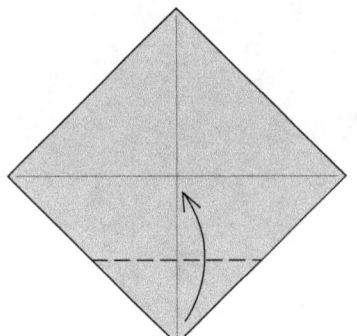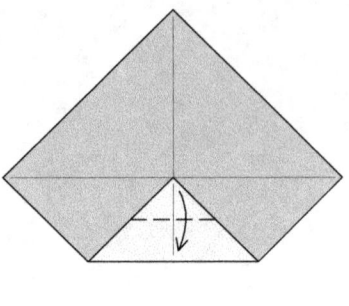

1. Precrease along the diagonals with a valley fold and a mountain fold.
2. Valley fold to the center.
3. Valley fold down to the edge.

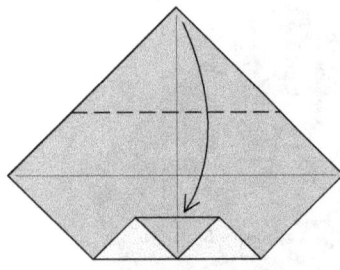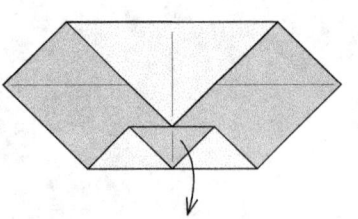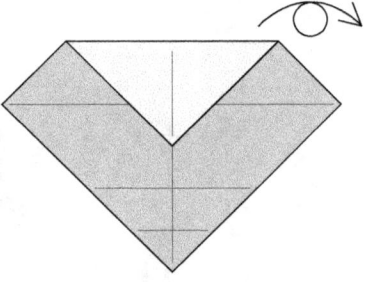

4. Valley fold the corner to the edge.
5. Unfold the bottom pleat.
6. Turn over.

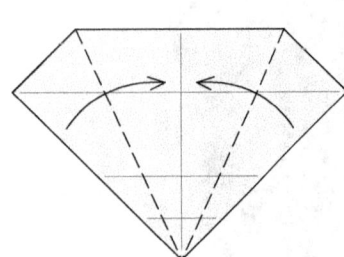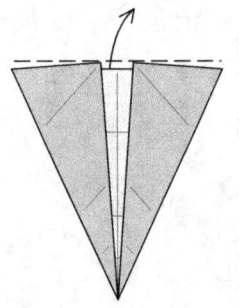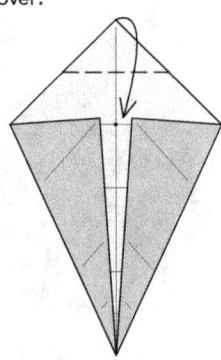

7. Valley fold the sides inwards.
8. Unfold the corner from behind.
9. Valley fold towards the dotted intersection of creases.

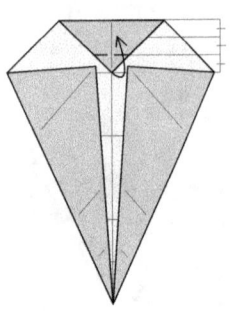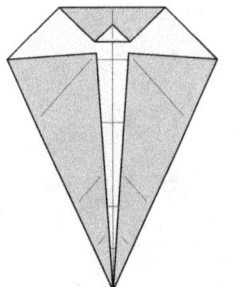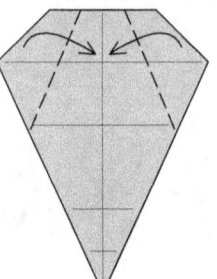

10. Valley fold the corner up along the 1/3rd division.
11. Turn over.
12. Valley fold the edges to the center.

skunk

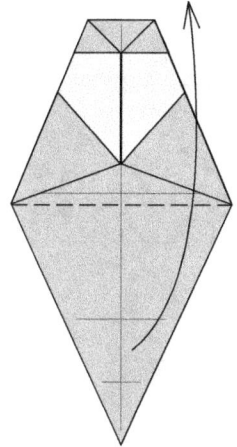

13. Valley fold the flap up.

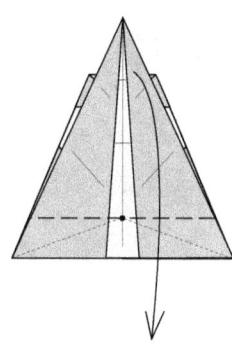

14. Valley fold down, aligning with the dotted hidden intersection.

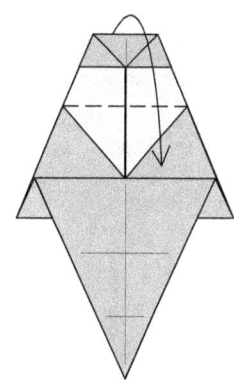

15. Valley fold down.

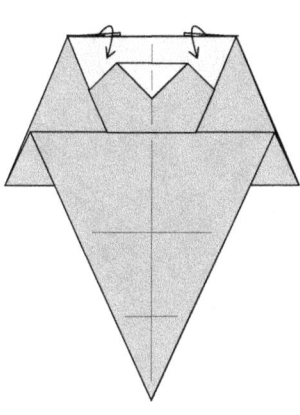

16. Valley fold the small corners down.

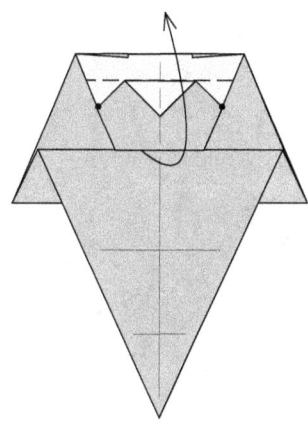

17. Valley fold up so the dotted corners hit the top edge.

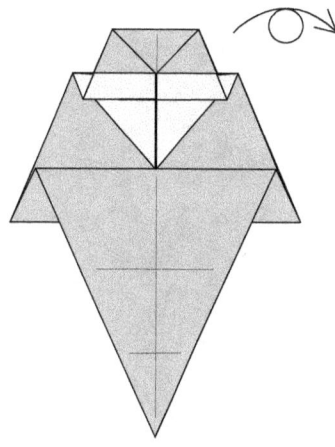

18. Turn over.

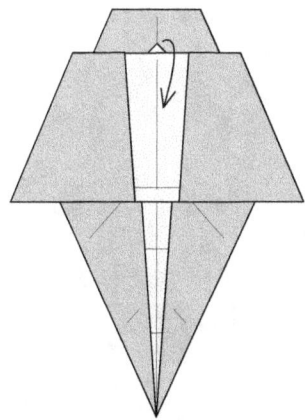

19. Pull the trapped flap out to the surface.

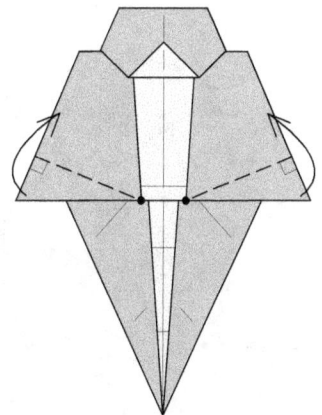

20. Starting from the dotted corners, valley fold the sides up.

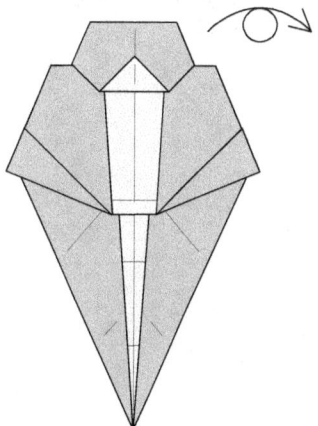

21. Turn over.

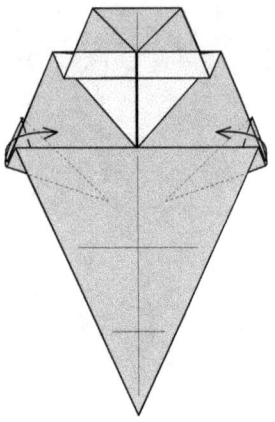

22. Valley fold the inner layers along the angle bisectors.

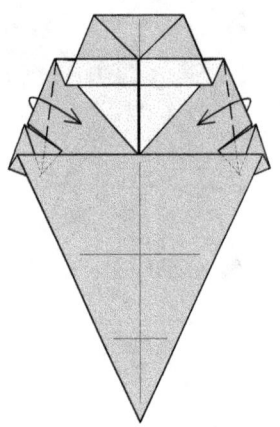

23. Valley fold the side edges inwards as far as possible.

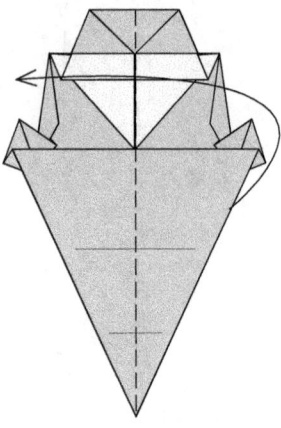

24. Valley fold the model in half.

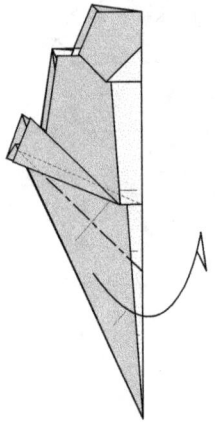

25. Mountain fold the flap allowing its edge to get tucked under the leg flap..

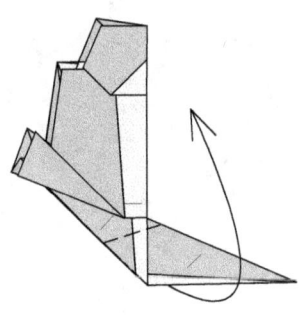

26. Valley fold the flap over. There are no reference points for this fold.

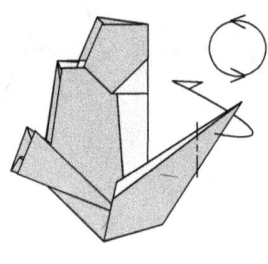

27. Mountain fold the corner. Rotate the model so it stands.

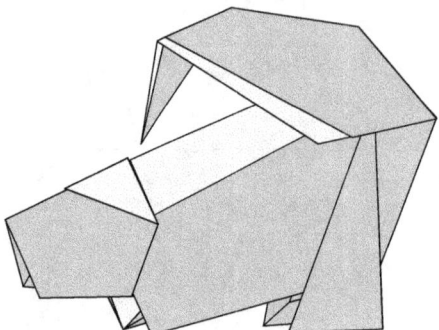

28. Completed *Skunk*.

Smiley Face

smiley face

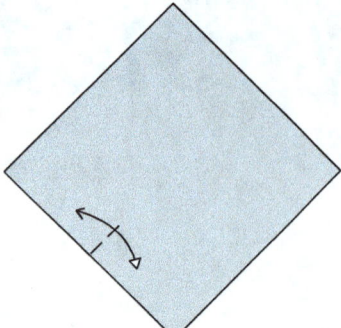

1. Precrease the edge in half.

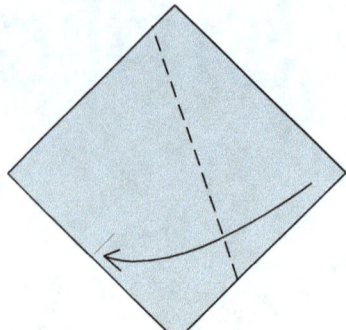

2. Valley fold the corner to the pinch mark.

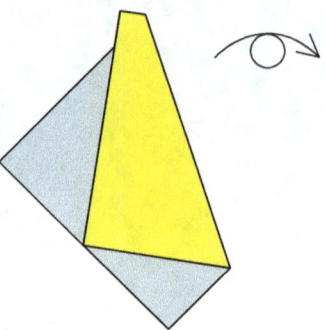

3. Turn over.

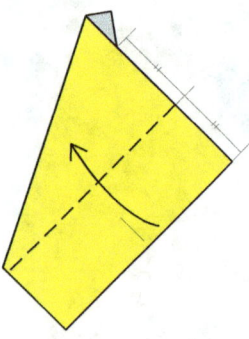

4. Valley fold so the corner hits the intersection.

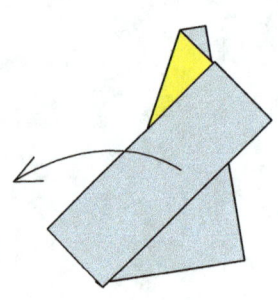

5. Unfold the pleat.

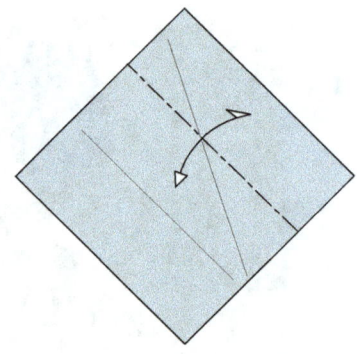

6. Precrease with a mountain fold.

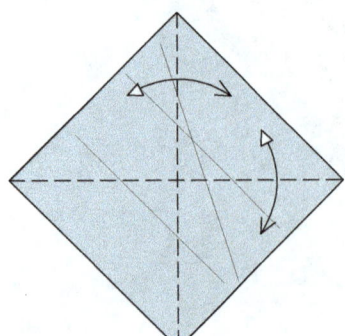

7. Precrease along the diagonals.

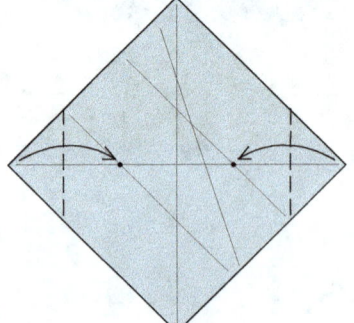

8. Valley fold the corners to the creases.

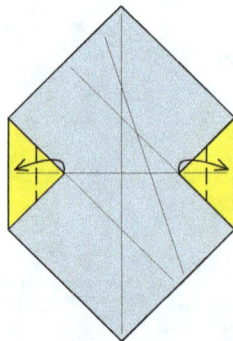

9. Valley fold the corners outwards.

smiley face

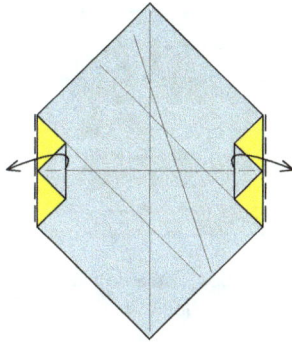

10. Swing the sides outwards.

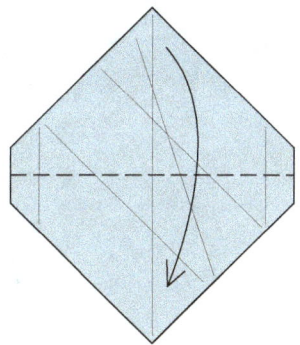

11. Valley fold in half.

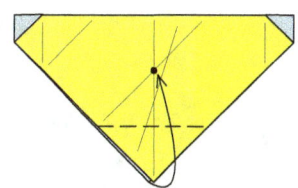

12. Valley fold both layers to the dotted intersection.

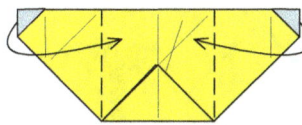

13. Valley fold the sides, allowing them to overlap.

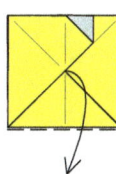

14. Swing the flaps down.

15. Turn over.

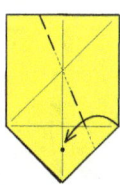

16. Valley fold so the corner hits the dotted crease. Try to avoid creasing the middle area.

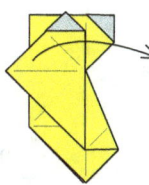

17. Note how the flap lies straight. Open out the pleat.

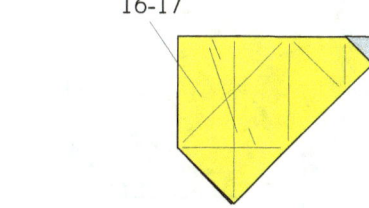

18. Repeat steps 16-17 in mirror image.

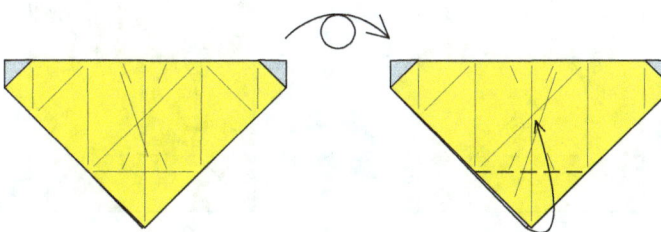

19. Turn over.

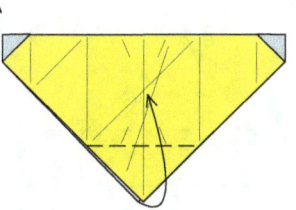

20. Valley fold the corners back up.

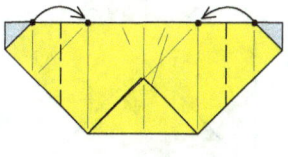

21. Valley fold the sides so the dotted parts meet.

smiley face

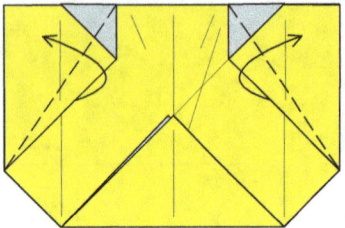

22. Valley fold the edges.

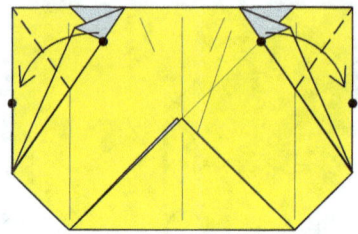

23. Valley fold the flaps so the dotted areas hit the outer dotted edges.

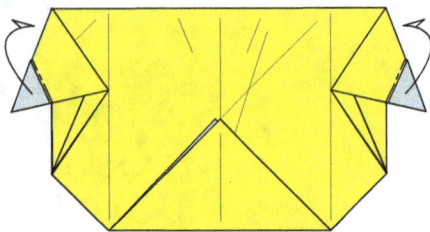

24. Mountain fold the colored corners behind.

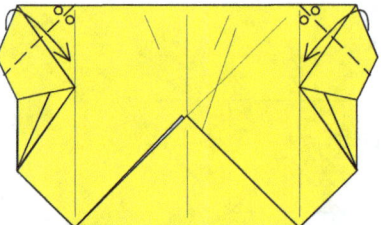

25. Valley fold along the indicated angle bisectors.

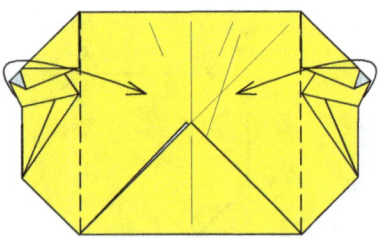

26. Valley fold the sides inwards.

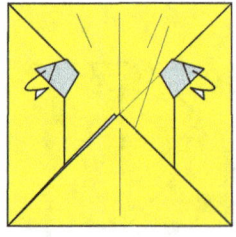

27. Mountain fold a little bit of the tips inside.

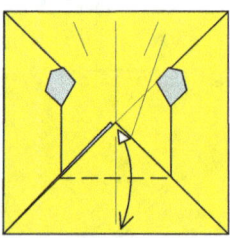

28. Precrease the top single layer in half.

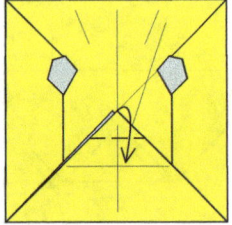

29. Valley fold to the last crease.

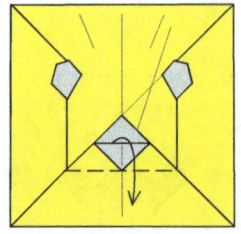

30. Valley fold along the existing crease.

31. Pinch the edge along the angle bisector.

104

smiley face

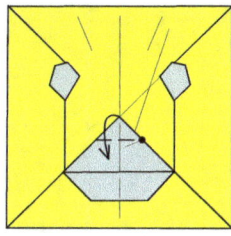

32. Valley fold starting from the dotted intercession.

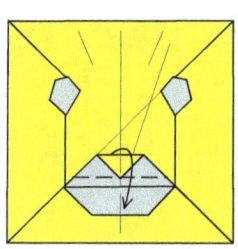

33. Valley fold the flap down partway.

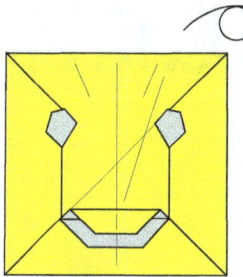

34. Turn over.

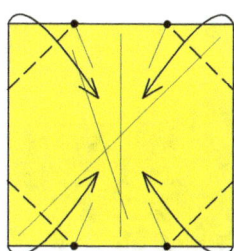

35. Valley fold the corners inwards using the dotted intersections as starting points.

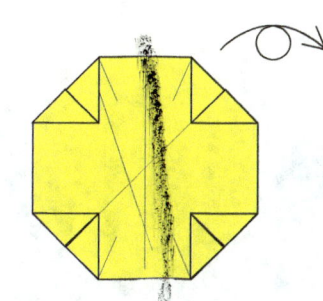

36. Turn over.

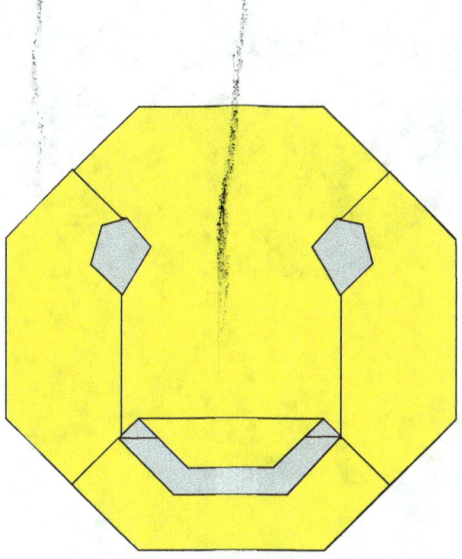

37. Completed *Smiley Face*.

105

Sunflower

sunflower

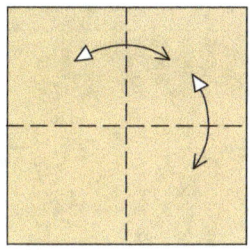

1. Precrease the sides in half.

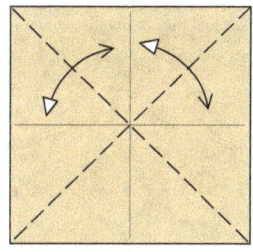

2. Precrease along the diagonals.

3. Valley fold the corners to the center.

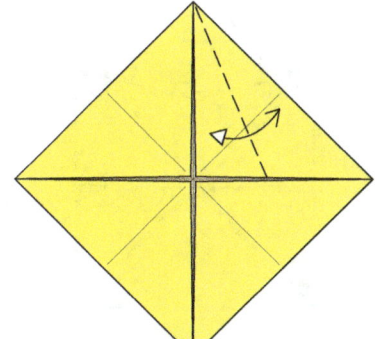

4. Precrease the top layer.

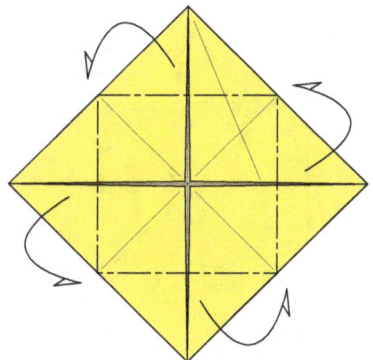

5. Mountain fold the corners behind. They will meet at the center.

6. Valley fold the top layer starting from the dotted intersection.

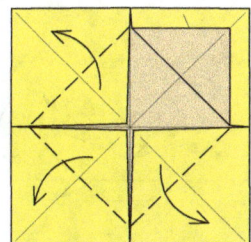

7. Valley fold the remaining corners outwards to match.

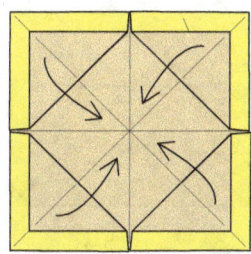

8. Bring the four corners back to the center.

9. Valley fold outwards towards the creases.

sunflower

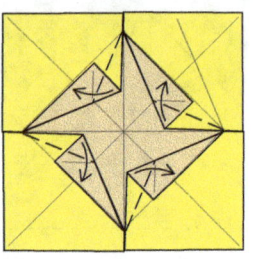
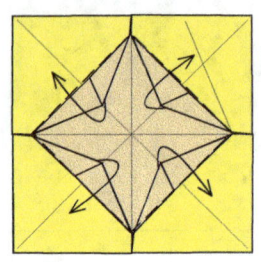
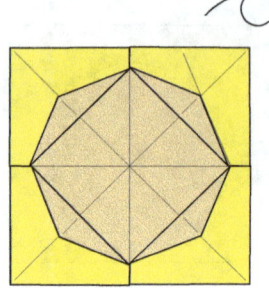

10. Valley fold the opposite edges towards the creases.

11. Valley fold the flaps outwards along the exiting creases.

12. Turn over.

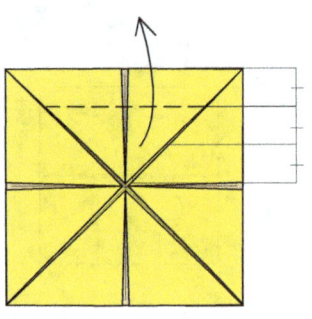
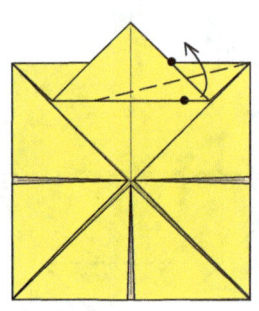
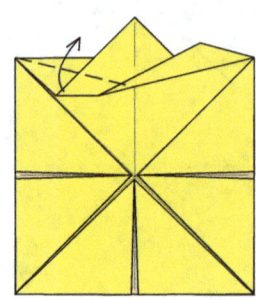

13. Valley fold the flap up at the 1/3rd mark.

14. Valley fold the edge up so the dotted edge hits the dotted corner.

15. Valley fold the opposite edge to match.

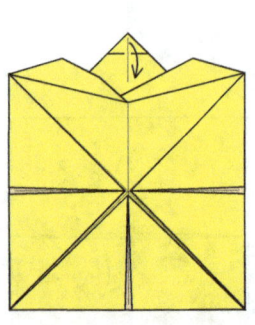
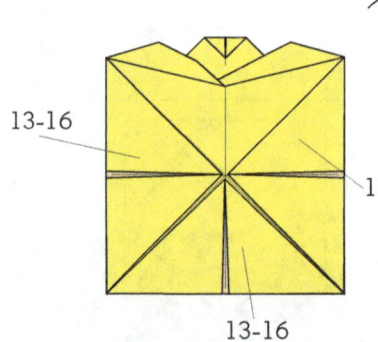

16. Valley fold the corner in partway.

17. Repeat steps 13-16 on the remaining three flaps. Turn over.

18. Completed *Sunflower*.

108

Teddy Bear

teddy bear

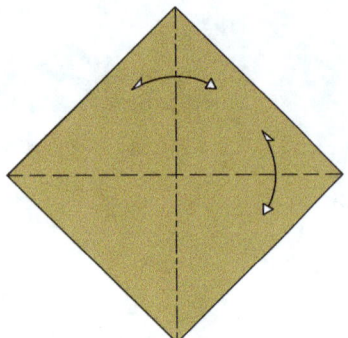

1. Precrease along the diagonals with mountain folds.

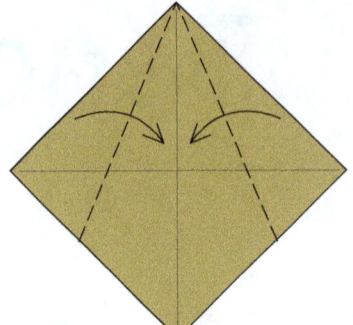

2. Valley fold to the center.

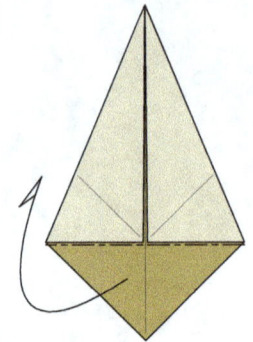

3. Mountain fold the bottom corner behind.

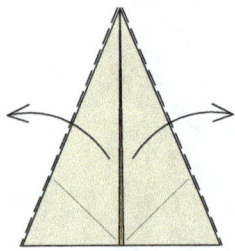

4. Open out the side flaps.

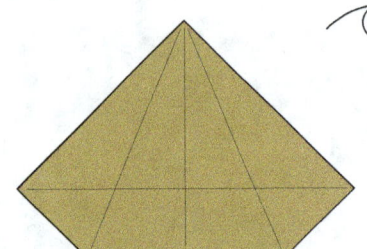

5. Turn over.

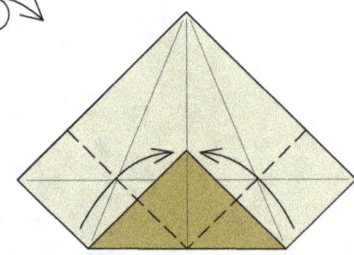

6. Valley fold the sides to the center.

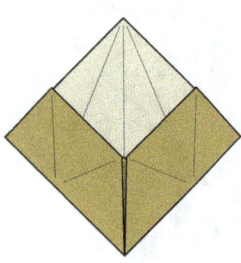

7. Turn over.

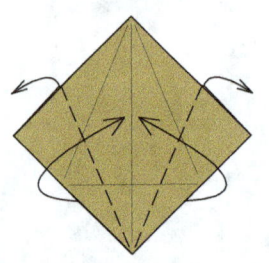

8. Valley fold the sides to the center, allowing the flaps from behind to swing forward.

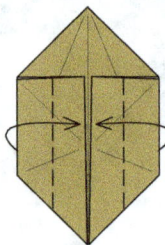

9. Valley fold the top layers to the center.

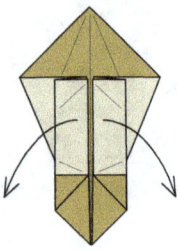

10. Open out the sides, leaving the last folds in place.

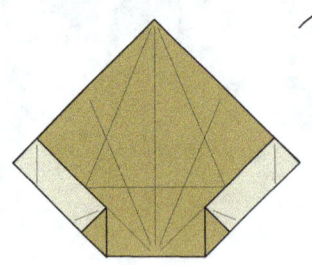

11. Turn over.

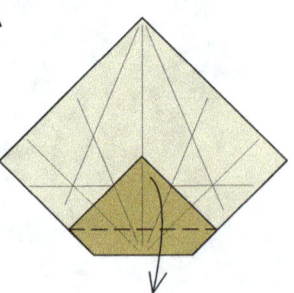

12. Valley fold the corner down.

teddy bear

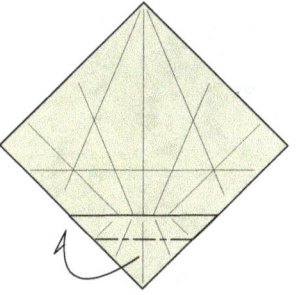

13. Mountain fold the corner around the hidden thick edge.

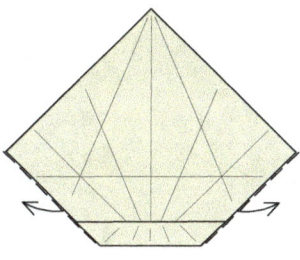

14. Unfold the sides from behind.

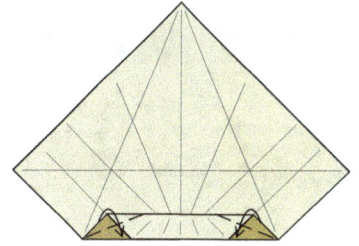

15. Valley fold along the angle bisectors.

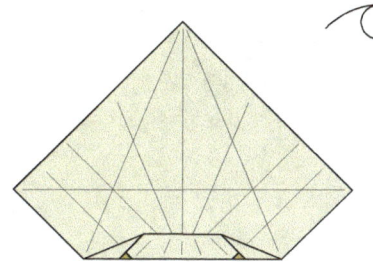

16. Turn over.

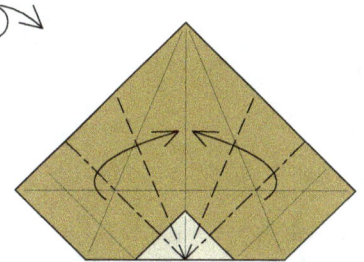

17. Reform the pleats at each side from steps 6-8.

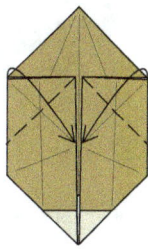

18. Valley fold the corners down.

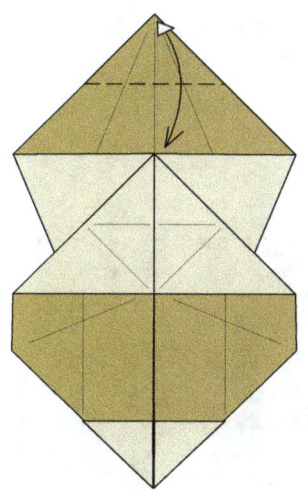

19. Precrease the top section in half.

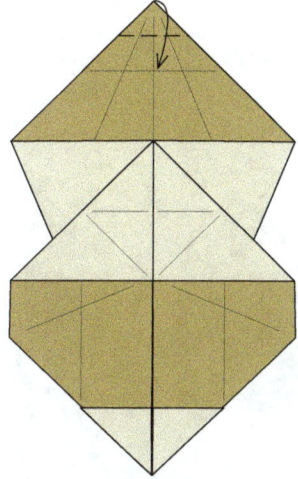

20. Valley fold to the last crease.

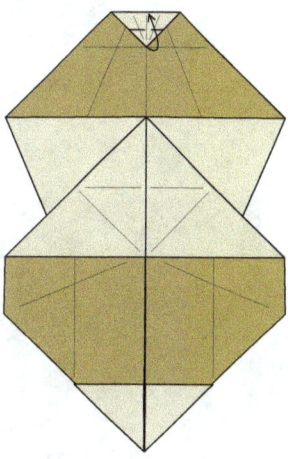

21. Valley fold up to the edge.

teddy bear

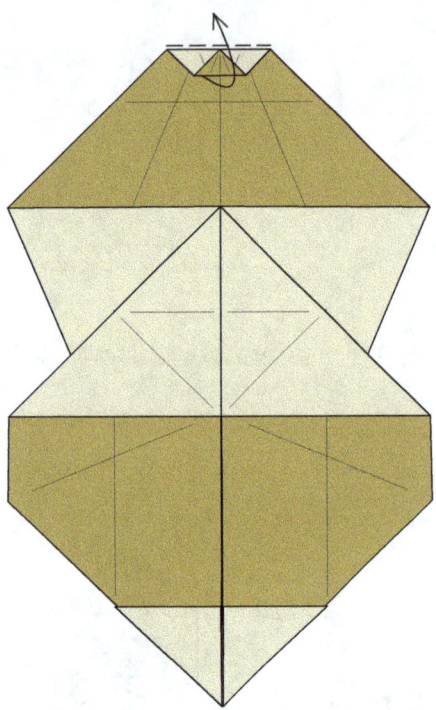

22. Open out the top, leaving the last fold in place.

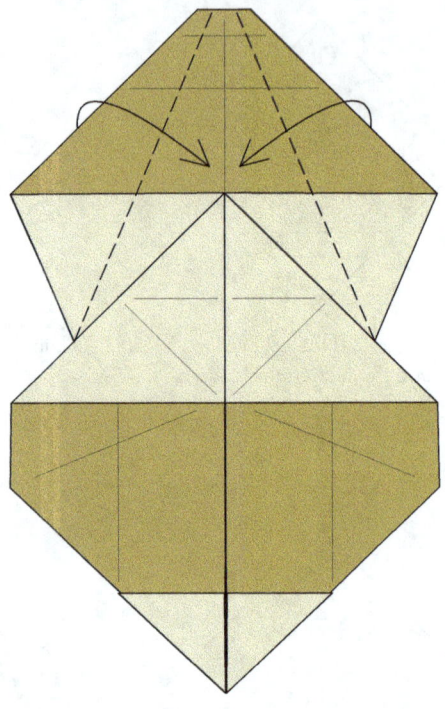

23. Valley fold the sides to the center.

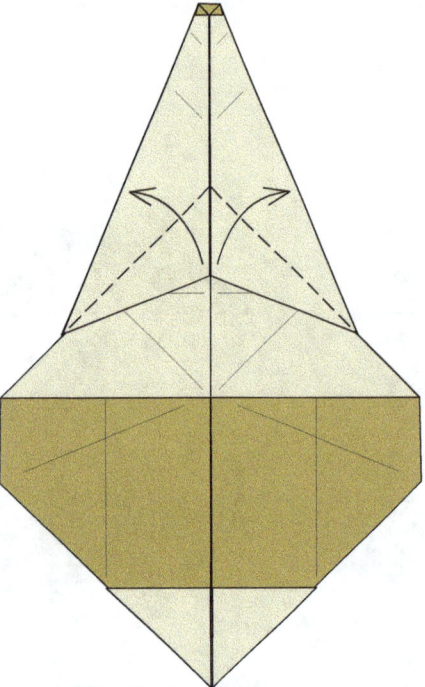

24. Valley fold to the outer edges.

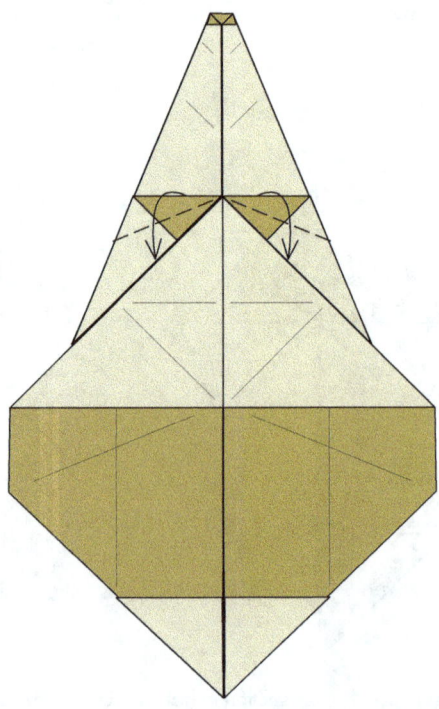

25. Valley fold along the angle bisectors.

teddy bear

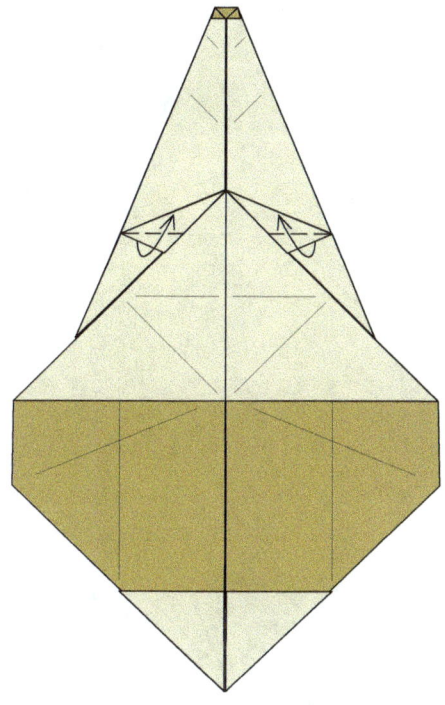

26. Valley fold the flaps up along the angle bisectors.

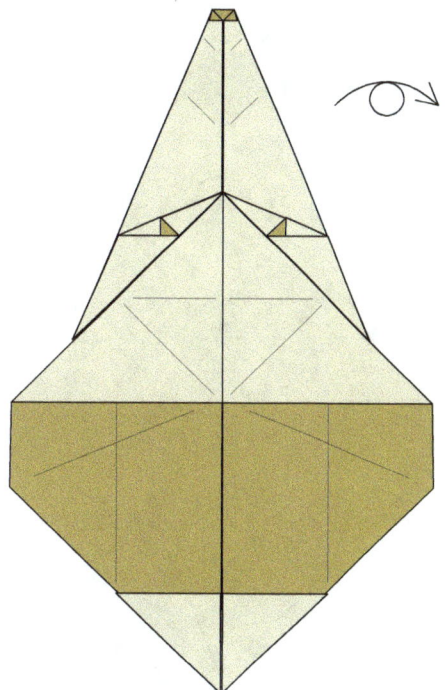

27. Turn over.

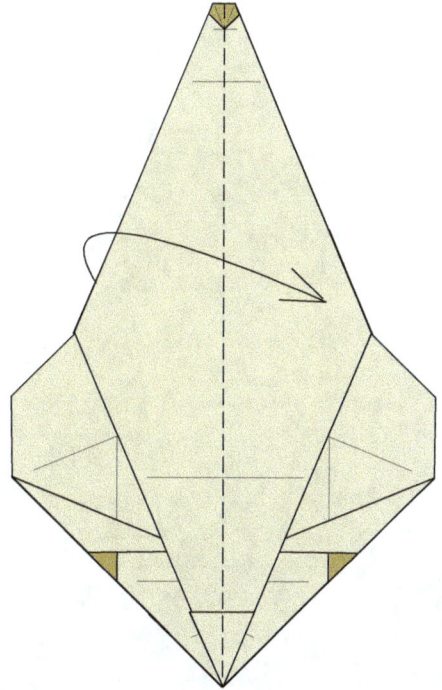

28. Swing over one flap.

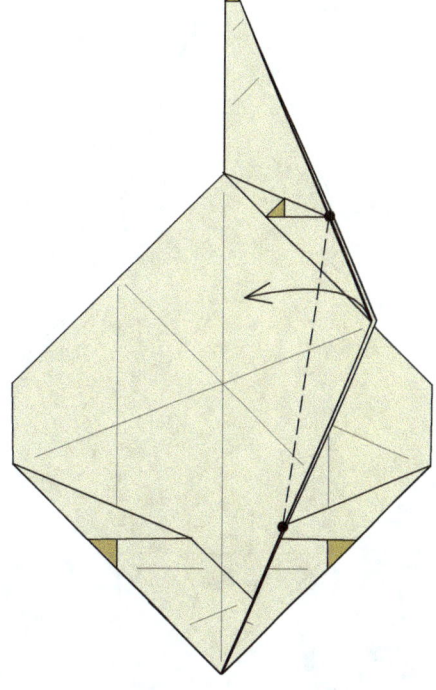

29. Form a valley fold between the dotted intersections.

teddy bear

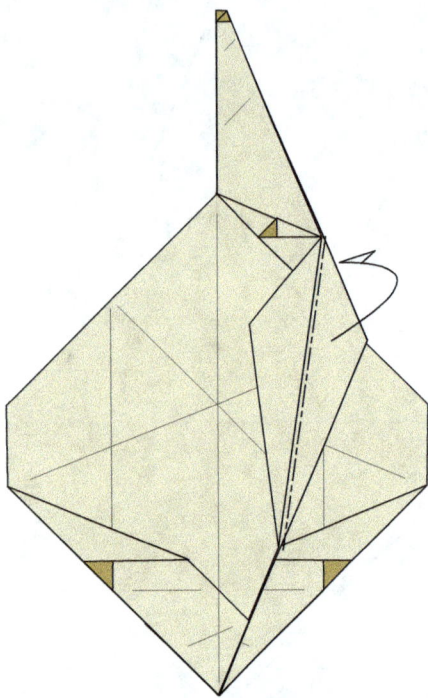

30. Mountain fold the layer behind to match the edge on the top layer.

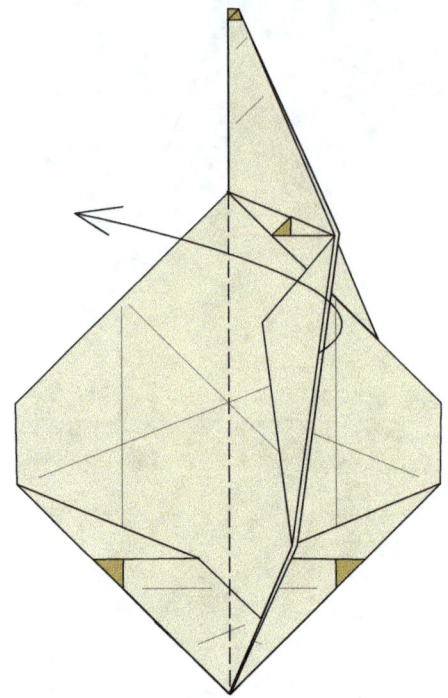

31. Swing over one flap.

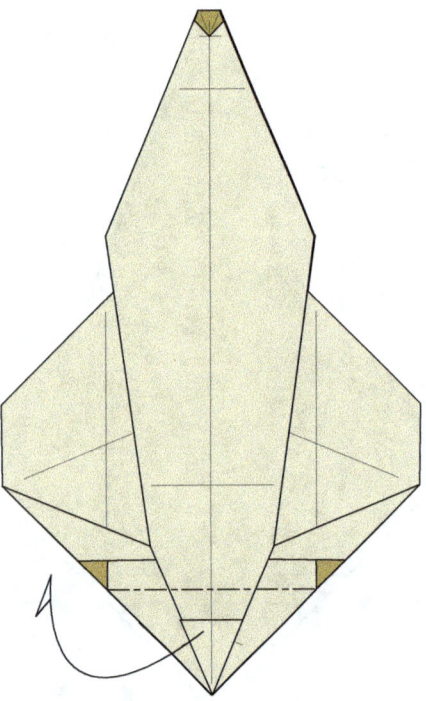

32. Mountain fold the bottom corner, aligning with the colored triangles.

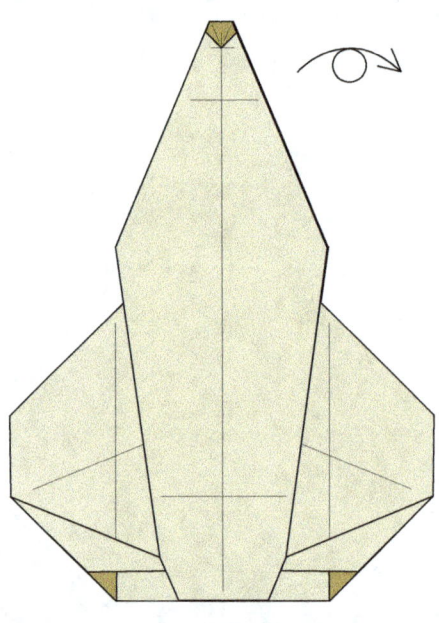

33. Turn over.

teddy bear

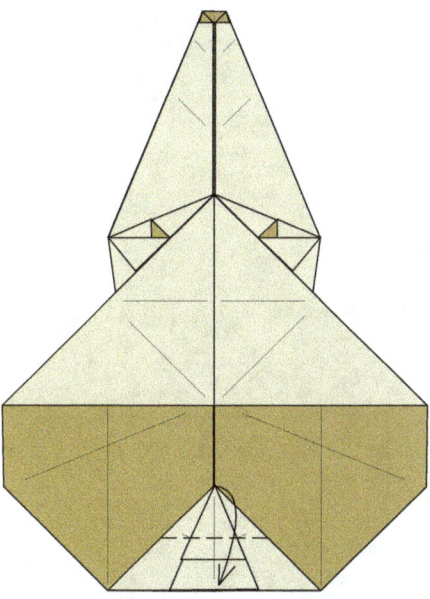

34. Valley fold the thick flap in half. It does not need to lie flat as it will act as a stand.

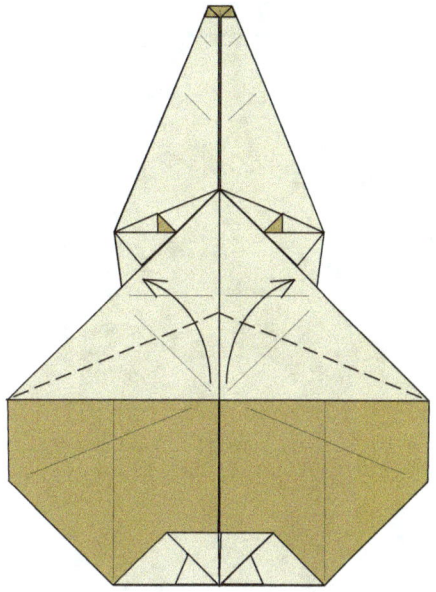

35. Valley fold the top layer.

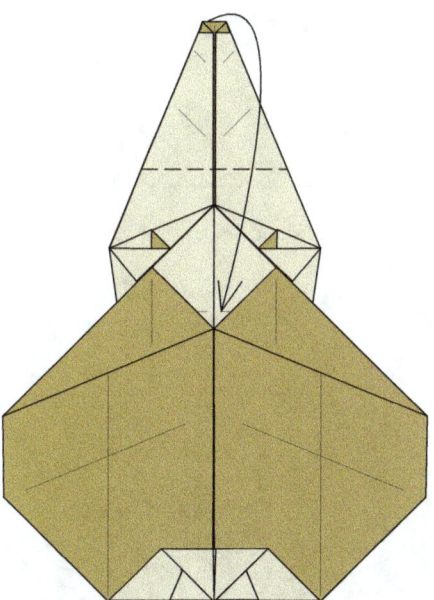

36. Valley fold the top flap so its corners hit the edges of the flaps.

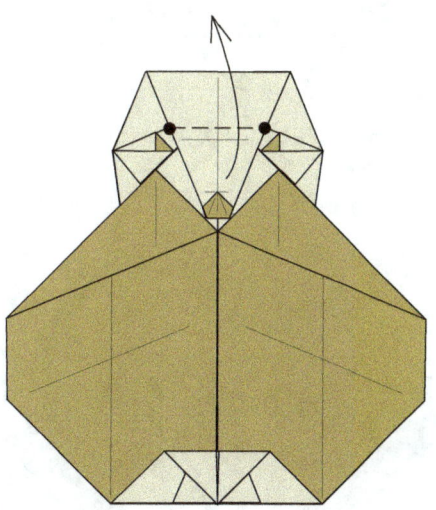

37. Valley fold noting the dotted intersections.

teddy bear

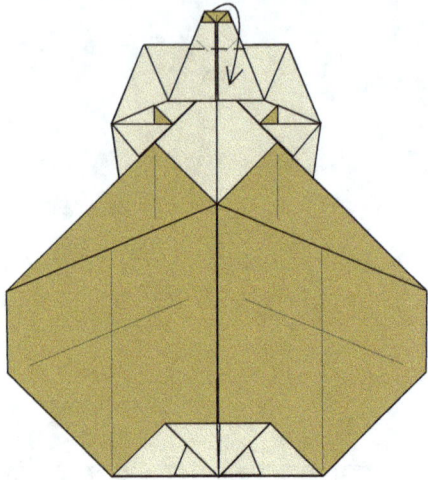

38. Valley fold so the colored tip lies in the middle of the flap.

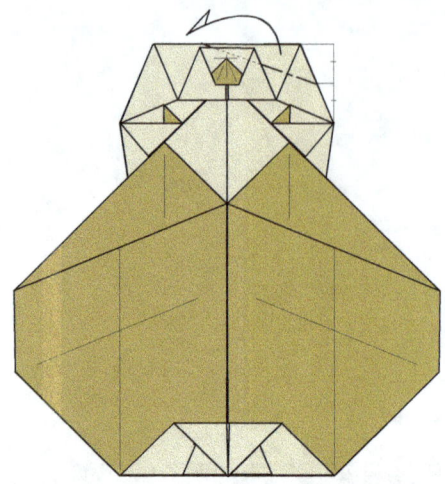

39. Mountain fold the edge, starting from the indicated halfway point.

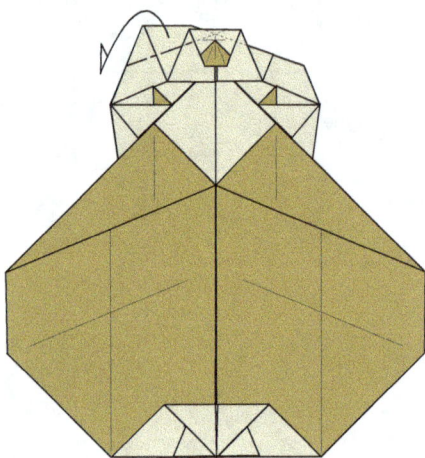

40. Mountain fold the other side to match. The layers will overlap behind.

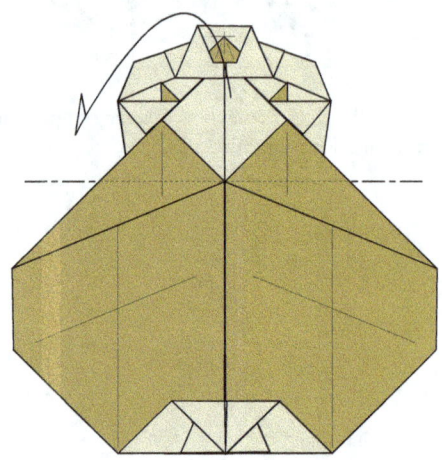

41. Mountain fold the top section behind.

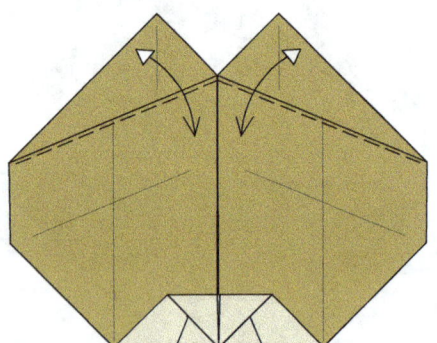

42. Precrease through all layers at each side. Turn over.

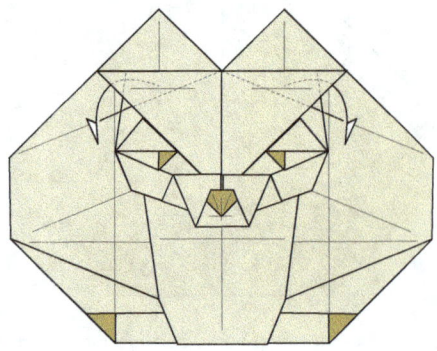

43. Using the existing creases, mountain fold the middle hidden layers.

teddy bear

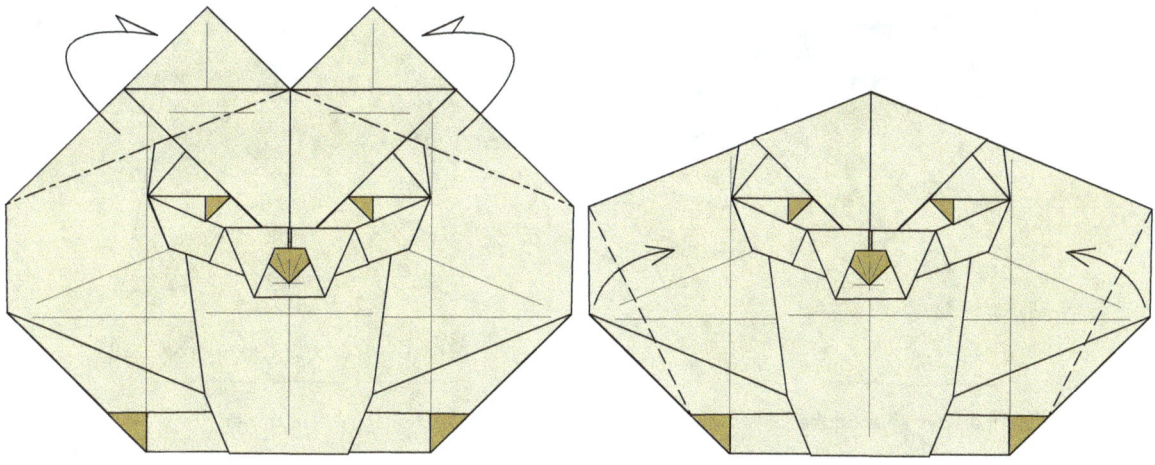

44. Mountain fold along the existing creases.

45. Valley fold the corners inwards.

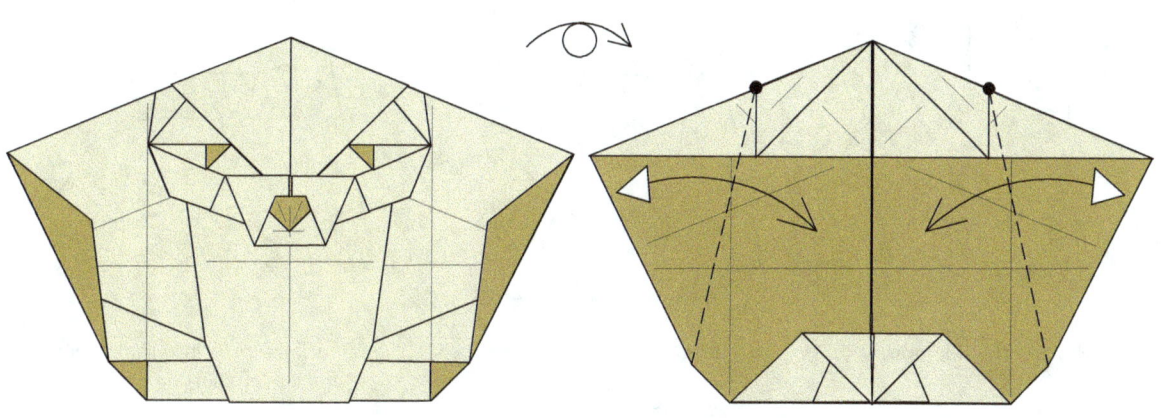

46. Turn over.

47. Precrease the side flaps, noting the dotted intersections.

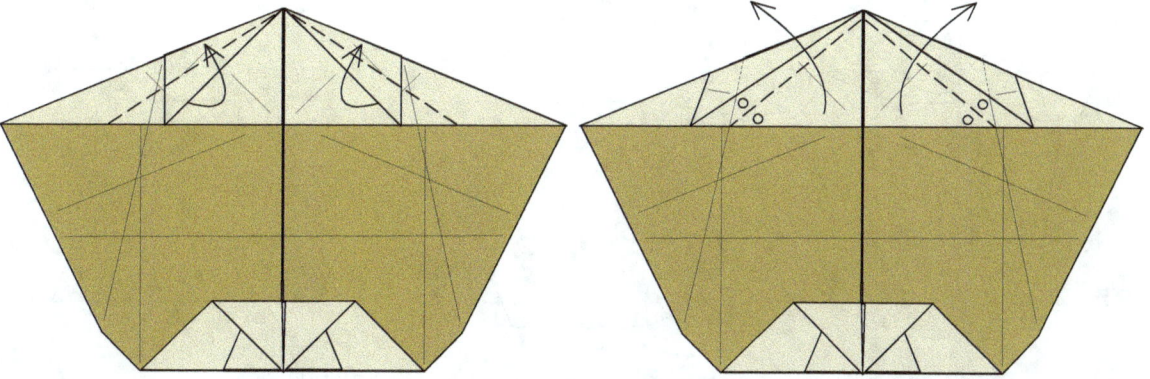

48. Valley fold along the angle bisectors.

49. Valley fold towards the creases from step 47, noting the indicated angle bisectors.

teddy bear

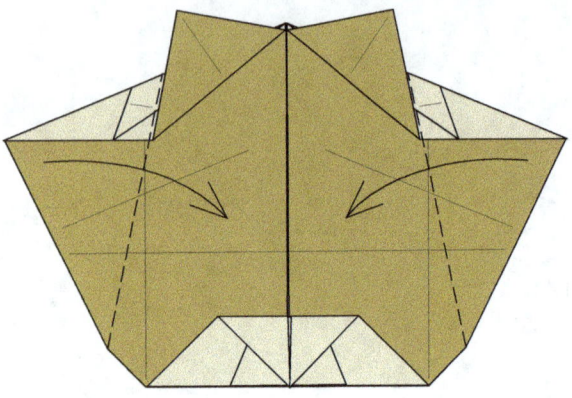

50. Valley fold the sides in along the folds from step 47.

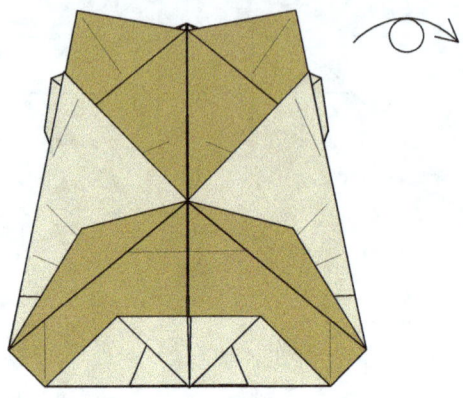

51. Turn over.

52. Valley fold the side over.

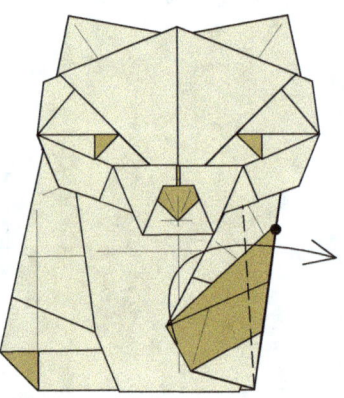

53. Valley fold the flap back out so its edge hits the dotted intersection.

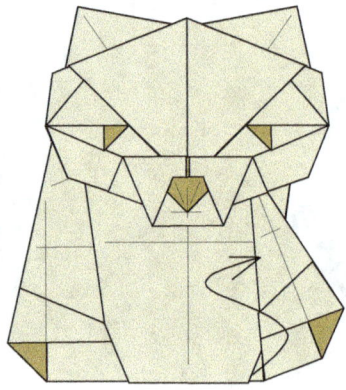

54. Tuck the resulting pleat under the center section.

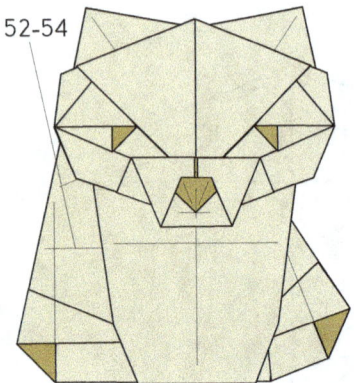

52-54

55. Repeat steps 52-54 in mirror image.

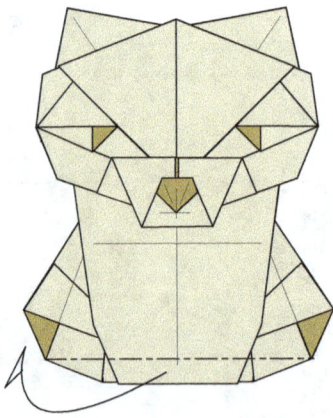

56. Mountain fold the bottom edge, aligning with the colored triangles.

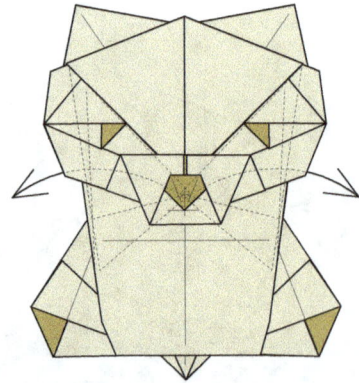

57. Fold the hidden flaps out partway. Look at the next step for approximate positioning.

teddy bear

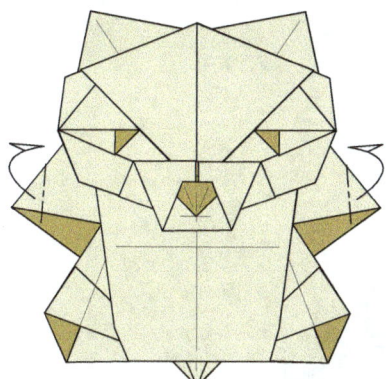

58. Mountain fold the tips of the flaps in partway.

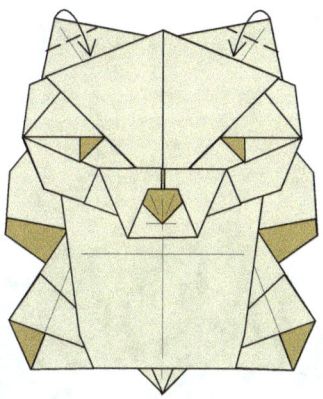

59. Valley fold the tips of the top flaps.

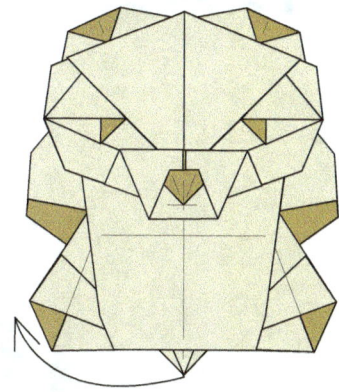

60. Pull the bottom flap back a bit so the model can stand.

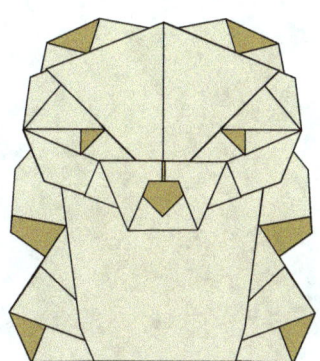

61. Completed *Teddy Bear*.

Tree

― tree ―

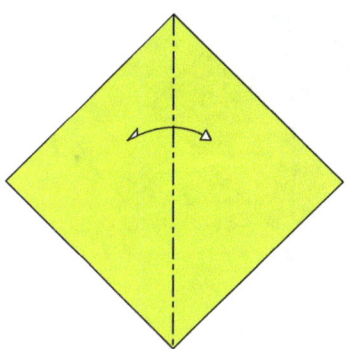

1. Precrease along the diagonal with a mountain fold.

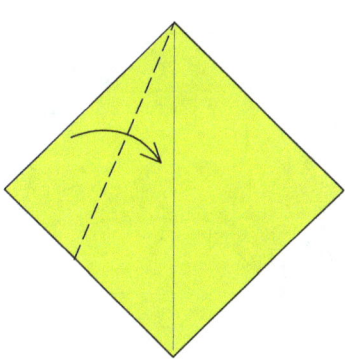

2. Valley fold the side to the center.

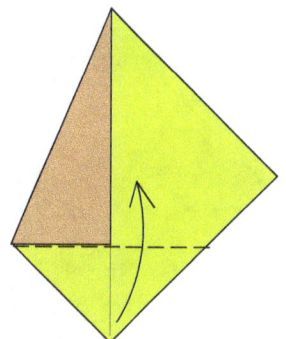

3. Valley fold the corner up.

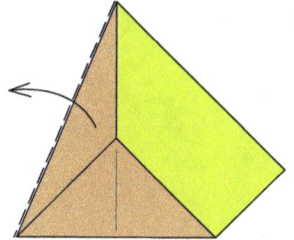

4. Open out the side flap.

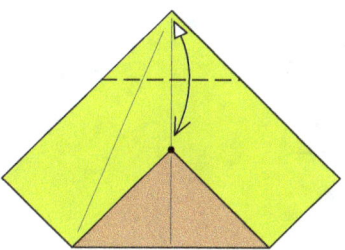

5. Precrease to the dotted corner.

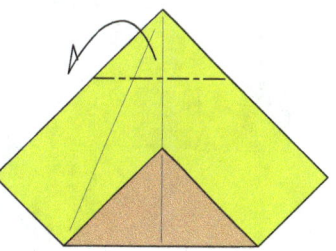

6. Mountain fold along the exiting crease.

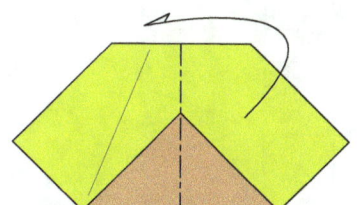

7. Mountain fold in half.

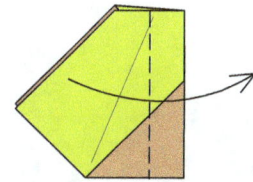

8. Valley fold so the top corners meet.

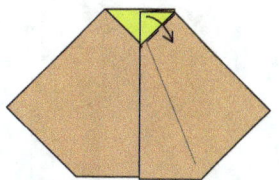

9. Valley fold the corner down.

tree

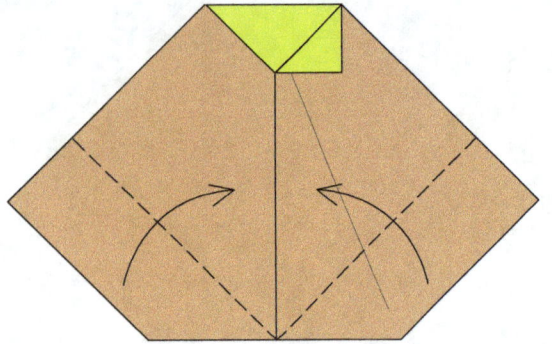

10. Valley fold the bottom edges up.

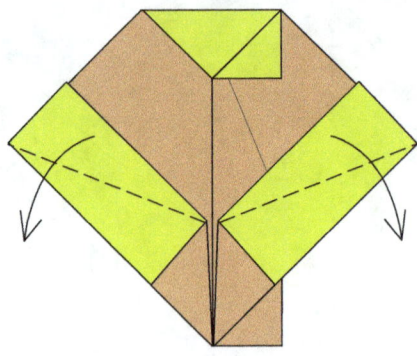

11. Valley fold the corners down.

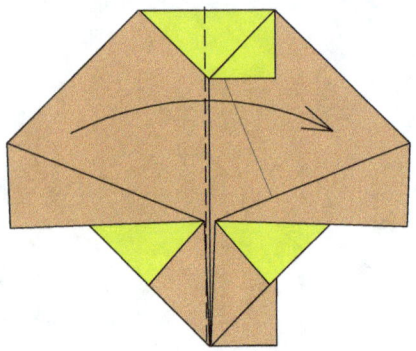

12. Valley fold in half.

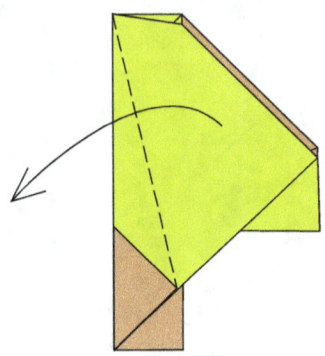

13. Valley fold the top layer over.

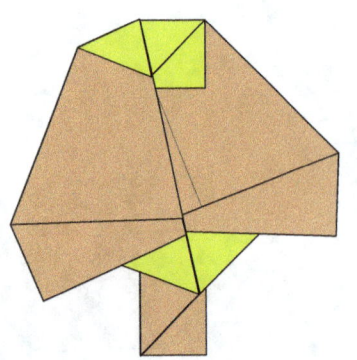

14. Turn over.

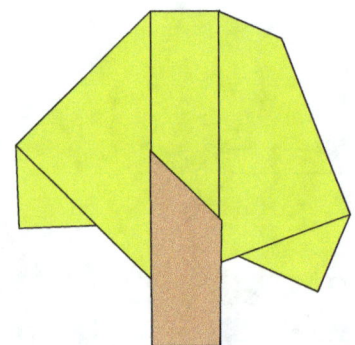

15. Completed *Tree*.

T-rex

t-rex

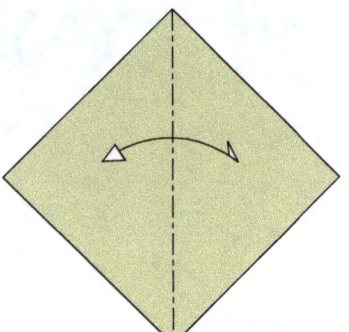

1. Precrease the diagonal with a mountain fold.

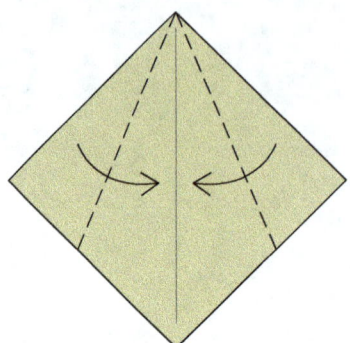

2. Valley fold the sides to the center.

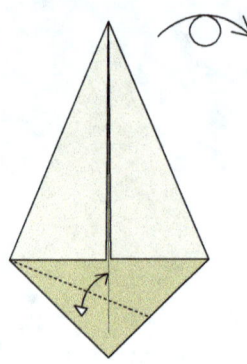

3. Pinch the center along the angle bisector. Turn over.

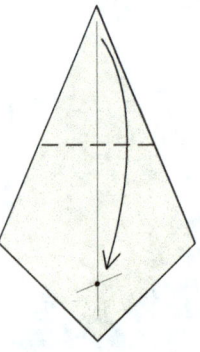

4. Valley fold to the dotted intersection of creases.

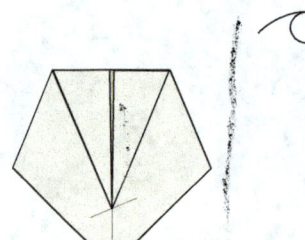

5. Turn over.

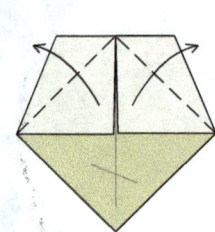

6. Valley fold the corners outwards as far as possible.

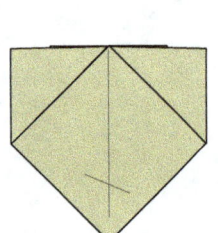

7. Turn over.

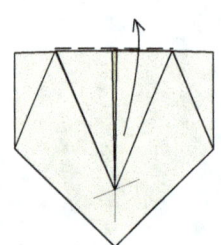

8. Raise the top flap.

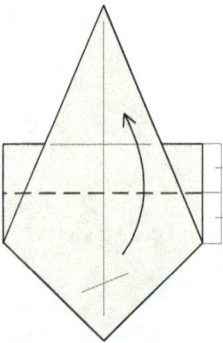

9. Valley fold the indicated section in half.

t - r e x

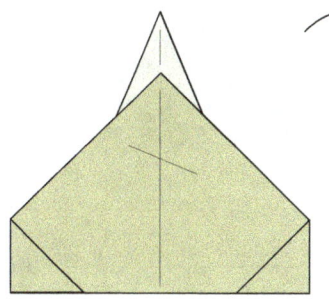

10. Turn over.

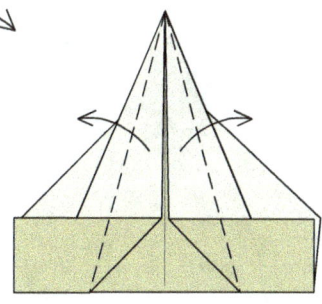

11. Valley fold the flaps outwards as far as possible.

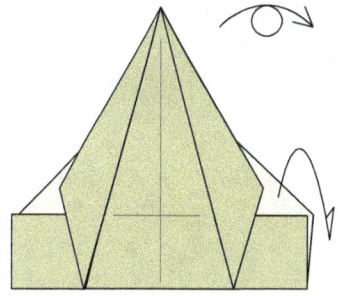

12. Swing down the back flap. Turn over.

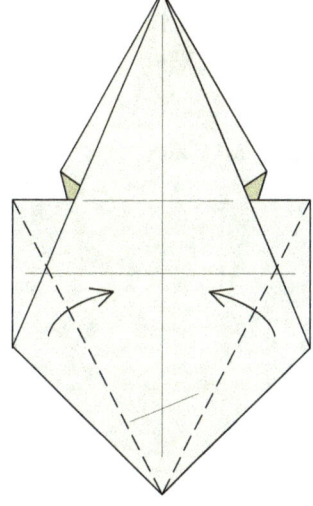

13. Valley fold the sides inwards from corner to corner.

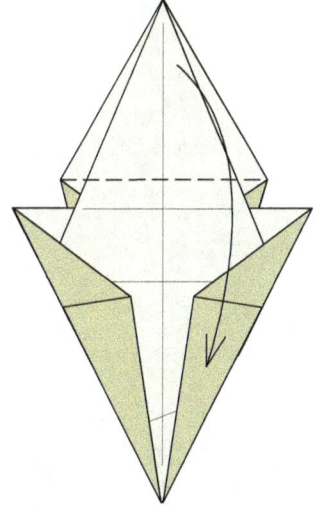

14. Valley fold the top flap down from corner to corner.

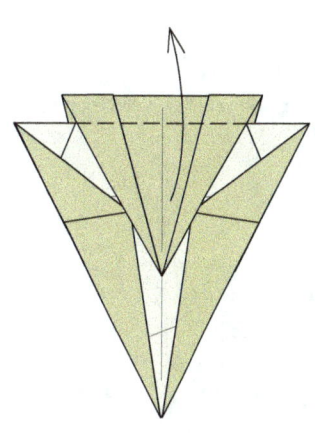

15. Valley fold the flap back up again, aligning with the side flaps.

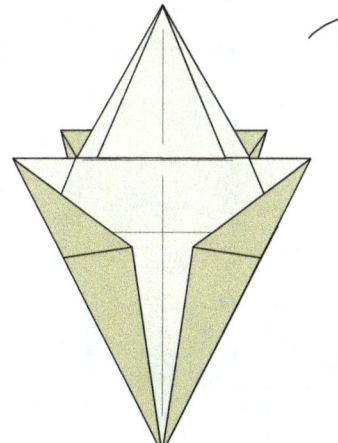

16. Turn over.

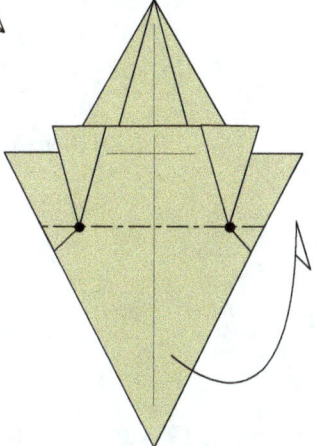

17. Mountain fold, aligning with the dotted corners.

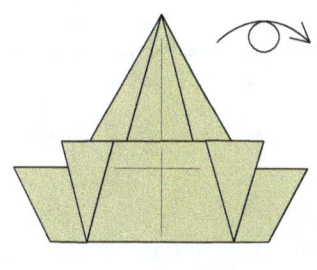

18. Turn over.

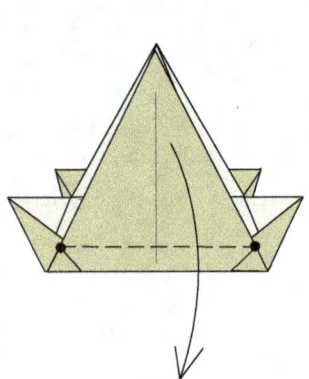

19. Valley fold the flap down, aligning with the dotted corners.

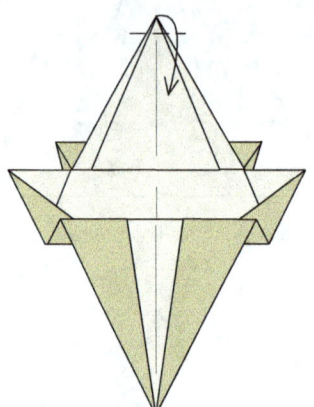

20. Valley fold a little bit of the tip in.

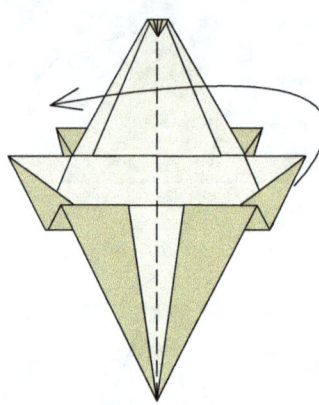

21. Valley fold in half.

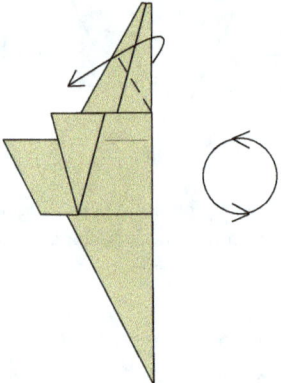

22. Valley fold the head over and rotate the model.

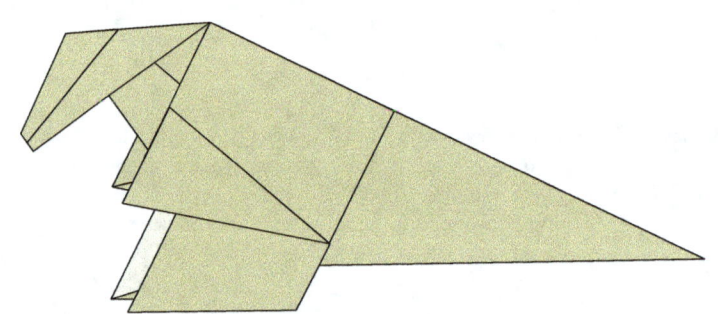

23. Completed *T-rex*.

www.ingramcontent.com/pod-product-compliance
Lightning Source LLC
Chambersburg PA
CBHW081750100526
44592CB00015B/2372